ELIAS MAMALAKIS

Cooking GREEK

hartini poli®

COOKING GREEK
ELIAS MAMALAKIS

APRIL 2023
ISBN: 978-960-621-874-3

Translation: El-translation

Editing: Angeliki Georgiakaki
Creative designer: Dimitra Zampoura - Angeliki Minadaki

HARTINI POLI EDITIONS ® a member of NAKAS GROUP
23rd km. Marathonos Ave. - Rafina 19009 - Attica • Tel.: 22940 79816
email: info@hartinipoli.gr • www.hartinipoli.gr
hartinipolieditions hartinipolibooks
hartinipoli Εκδόσεις Χάρτινη Πόλη

ELIAS MAMALAKIS

Cooking GREEK

95 traditional recipes
from Greece

Dear friends,

My name is **Elias Mamalakis,** I am a cook and I deal exclusively with the traditional Greek cuisine.

My country is surrounded by the Mediterranean Sea and its coastline spans across seventeen thousand kilometers. So, our cuisine includes plenty of fish and seafood.

On the other hand, however, there are many plains on the mainland, where cereals are grown (wheat, barley, oats and corn), while many herds graze in the high mountains, mainly with sheep and goats.

Many of our products in Greece have a Protected Designation of Origin (PDO), such as Feta cheese, Naxos graviera cheese, Kalathaki Limnou cheese, as well as mastic from Chios, saffron, pistachio from Aegina, olive oil and table olives. This means that these products have unique quality characteristics, which are linked to their geographical origin as well as traditional know-how.

The Greek diet was based on **3 staples**: bread, wine and olive oil.

It was here that the standard of the Mediterranean diet was born, mainly on the island of Crete. A diet that includes plenty of cereals, fruits, vegetables, dairy, eggs and minimal meat. You see, Greece formed its diet through simple recipes with ingredients that nature offers in abundance. And that is why in fact, many of the recipes are not only vegetarian but vegan.

In every region of Greece, their cuisine relies on local ingredients. Thus, the same recipe can change drastically from region to region.

For example, in Epirus, which has a lot of dairy products, pies have lots of cheese and less phyllo pastry. On the contrary, in Thessaly, which produces a lot of wheat, pies are rich in phyllo pastry and contain less cheese.

In our country, the so-called urban cuisine emerged in the 19th century, and many of its recipes are cooked all over Greece. A typical example is the famous moussaka, as well as the Greek salad.

In this book I am **presenting 95** sweet and savory traditional recipes, which I collected along my journeys even to the most remote areas of Greece, in an effort to combine taste with culture.

I handpicked the recipes so that you can easily find all of the ingredients.

I hope that my book will serve as your guide to a mouthwatering and nutritious diet and transport you to my wonderful country.

Elias Mamalakis

CONTENTS

RECIPES from all over GREECE

SALADS-SPREADS

MAIN DISHES

DESSERTS

RECIPES from GRETE

RECIPES from CYCLADES ISLANDS

RECIPES from PELOPONNESE

RECIPES
from all over
GREECE

While some recipes may have originated in a particular region, it is true that they quickly gained national popularity. Salads and dips, main dishes with meat and seafood, as well as «ladera» dishes, made with vegetables and legumes and, of course, extra-virgin olive oil, as well as desserts -primarily syrup and spoon sweets- are prepared throughout Greece and constitute the foundation of the Greek diet.

Delicious wine, smooth tsipouro or aromatic ouzo accompany the flavorful, tradition-rich, and lovingly prepared dishes that are served on tables across the country.

So begins our tour of the creative, delicious, and healthy cuisine of Greece!

POLITIKI *salad*

for 1 large salad bowl

Ingredients

- *½ kg white cabbage, finely shredded*
- *3 carrots, grated*
- *4 celery stalks, without the leaves, finely chopped*
- *2 garlic cloves, finely chopped*
- *1 red pickled pepper (Florina pepper)*
- *2 tablespoons vinegar*
- *juice of 1 lemon*
- *salt*
- *olive oil*
- *olives for garnishing*

- Put the cabbage, carrots, celery and garlic inside a large bowl.
- Salt them well, pour over the lemon juice and ¼ cup of water, mix and let marinate for 1 hour.
- Drain the salad from its liquids, put in a salad bowl, finely chop the Florina pepper, pour over the vinegar, drizzle with as much olive oil as you want, garnish with olives and serve.

The longer the salad is left to sit, the more delicious it becomes, as it acquires a slightly pickled taste.

GREEK *salad*

for 1 large salad bowl

Ingredients
- *3 large ripe tomatoes*
- *1 cucumber with its peel*
- *1 large onion cut into thin rounds*
- *2 green peppers cut into rounds*
- *¼ cup capers*
- *1 cup Kalamata olives*
- *1 tablespoon oregano*
- *½ cup olive oil*
- *¼ cup vinegar*
- *250 g Feta cheese cut into cubes*
- *salt*

- Wash all the vegetables thoroughly.
- Remove the stem from the tomatoes and cut them into slices.
- Cut the cucumber, the onion and the pepper into rounds and toss the salad with two spoons.
- Add the olives, salt, oregano, vinegar and olive oil.
- Mix well and add the Feta cheese.
- Mix gently and transfer to a salad bowl.

The biggest secret to a delicious Greek salad is mixing it well. My late grandmother used to say that a good Greek salad needs you to be generous with the oil, miserly with the vinegar and a madman when you mix it.

TZATZIKI

for 1 large bowl

Ingredients

- 1 kg Greek yoghurt
- ¼ cup olive oil
- 2 tablespoons vinegar
- 1 large cucumber (with the peel)
- 4 garlic cloves
- 1 cup dill, finely chopped
- ¼ cup spearmint, finely chopped
- salt

for garnishing

- 2 tablespoons olive oil
- some black olives

- Wash the cucumber well, cut off its ends and coarsely grate it on the grater.
- Lightly salt it and leave in a colander for about 15 minutes. Then squeeze it very well, until completely dry.
- Put the yoghurt in a large bowl, put in the cucumber and mix well.
- Crush the garlic and add it to the yoghurt mixture. Stir well and add the olive oil and vinegar.
- Lightly salt, add the dill and spearmint and stir again.
- Serve in bowl, drizzle with a little olive oil and garnish with black olives.

SKORDALIA

for 1 large bowl

Ingredients

- *6 garlic cloves*
- *3 thick slices of stale bread without the crust*
- *1 tablespoon lemon*
- *2 tablespoons vinegar*
- *olive oil, as much as needed*
- *a little salt*

- Soak the bread in water. Once it softens, squeeze out the water with your hands and crumble it.
- Put the garlic into the food processor with some salt, and crush into a smooth pulp.
- Add the bread gradually, together with ¼ cup of water, constantly working the processor until it has reached a homogeneous consistency.
- Add the vinegar, lemon, a little salt and the olive oil, until it emulsifies into a mixture as smooth as mayonnaise.
- Put the garlic sauce into a bowl and serve.

*Skordalia is an ideal **accompaniment** for fried fish and **seafood**, as well as boiled salads.*

TYROKAFTERI

for 1 bowl

Ingredients

- *150 g anthotyro cheese or ricotta cheese*
- *150 g Katiki Domokou or cream cheese*
- *150 g Feta cheese*
- *3 tablespoons olive oil*
- *1 hot green pepper, finely chopped*
- *freshly ground pepper*
- *5-6 drops Tabasco*

- Put all the ingredients in the food processor, except the pepper, and blend them until they become a homogeneous paste.
- Put the contents into a bowl and mix with the pepper.
- Serve on an oval platter and accompany with fresh bread.

Tyrokafteri is one of the favourite appetizers of the Greeks, as it is spicy and refreshing at the same time.

TARAMOSALATA

for 1 bowl

Ingredients

- *100 g white fish roe*
- *150 g stale bread (without the crust)*
- *1 small onion, blended into a pulp*
- *3 cups olive oil*
- *½ cup lemon juice*

for garnishing

- *some black olives*
- *onion slices*
- *some dill*

- Soak the bread in water, squeeze it very well, crumble it with your hands and knead it with the fish roe.
- Put the onion and the fish roe mixture in a blender and blend together.
- Continue blending, slowly pour in the oil, alternating with the lemon juice.
- When it turns into a smooth paste, transfer to a platter or bowl and garnish with onion slices and dill.

Taramosalata is also delicious if you blend the fish roe only with the oil, onion and lemon, without the bread. You will need more oil, but it is worth it.

Fish roe (taramas) are the well-salted eggs of cod.

RUSSIAN *salad*

for 1 large bowl

Ingredients

- *4 large potatoes*
- *4 medium carrots*
- *1 cup fine peas*
- *6 pickled cucumbers, finely chopped*
- *4 tablespoons fine capers*
- *500 g mayonnaise*
- *juice of 1 lemon*
- *¼ cup olive oil*
- *salt, white pepper*

for garnishing

- *some olives*
- *1 boiled egg*

- Mix the mayonnaise with the olive oil and lemon juice, season with salt and pepper and place the mixture in the refrigerator.
- Peel the potatoes and carrots and boil them until they soften. Let them cool and cut into cubes.
- Scald the peas in boiling water for 1 minute. Drain and let it dry.
- In a large bowl add the potatoes, carrots, peas, pickled cucumbers, capers and mix. Add about half of the mayonnaise and stir gently to combine well with the other ingredients. Continue stirring, adding another 2-3 tablespoons of mayonnaise.
- Season with salt and pepper, drizzle with the lemon juice and mix.
- Put the Russian salad in a platter, spread it well with a fork and spread the rest of the mayonnaise over it evenly.
- Garnish with olives and the boiled egg.

MELITZANOSALATA *(aubergine salad)*

for 1 large bowl

Ingredients

- *3 globe aubergines, as large as possible*
- *½ green pepper*
- *½ tomato without the skin and seeds*
- *1 green onion*
- *¼ cup parsley, finely chopped*
- *some olive oil*
- *some vinegar*
- *salt*
- *2 garlic gloves*

- Preheat the oven at 200°C with the grill on. Put the aubergines in the oven and leave them until their peel burns and they start to shrink. Pierce them with a knife and if you do not find resistance they are ready.
- Remove them from the heat and let them cool. Take the peels off and put their flesh in a colander. Let all the liquids drain out for half an hour.
- Finely chop the aubergines, pepper, tomato and green onion.
- Put the pieces in a bowl, add the parsley and mix with a wooden spoon.
- Add salt, olive oil, a little vinegar, mix well and let the aubergine salad set in the refrigerator.

DOLMADAKIA *yialantzi*

for 50-60 stuffed vine leaves

Ingredients

- *60 tender vine leaves, blanched in salted water*
- *½ kg rice ('carolina')*
- *1½ cups olive oil*
- *½ cup pine nuts*
- *½ cup black raisins*
- *½ kg onions, finely chopped in the food processor*
- *¼ cup spearmint, finely chopped*
- *¼ cup dill, finely chopped*
- *salt, pepper*

for cooking

- *1 cup olive oil*
- *juice of 2 lemons*

Dolmadakia can be eaten both hot and cold and are often served with Greek yogurt.

- Heat the olive oil in a deep frying pan, sauté the onions until glossy and add the pine nuts and raisins.
- Sauté the ingredients over medium heat and add the rice after first rinsing it well.
- Season with salt and pepper, add the spearmint, dill, 2 cups of water, stir well and slowly simmer for 5 minutes.
- Remove the pan from the heat and let the filling "rest" for 10 minutes.
- Put the vine leaves on a clean surface, one at a time, place 1 teaspoon of filling in the centre, fold the sides inwards and roll to shape the dolma.
- Place the stuffed vine leaves next to each other in a pot, with the joint facing downwards and in layers.
- Add 1 cup olive oil, put a plate over the stuffed vine leaves to keep them in place, and add lukewarm water until nearly covered.
- Cook over medium heat for about half an hour until the rice is cooked.
- Remove from heat and drizzle the lemon juice over them.

IMAM *bayildi*

for 5-6 people

Ingredients

- *Long aubergines, cut in half (as many as you can fit in a baking pan)*
- *1 kg onions cut into matchsticks*
- *150 g olive oil*
- *20 g sweet paprika*
- *40 g parsley, finely chopped*
- *2 garlic cloves, finely chopped*
- *600 g tomato juice*
- *10 g sugar*
- *salt, pepper*

- Cut the aubergines lengthwise, rinse them with plenty of water and place in a pan. Brush them with oil and salt very lightly. Bake them in the oven until soft.
- In the meantime, prepare the stuffing: Heat the olive oil in a saucepan and sauté the onions and garlic until glossy. Add the parsley, paprika and stir.
- Add the tomato juice, sugar, salt and pepper. Cook for 2-3 minutes and remove the pot from the heat.
- Place the filling on the baked aubergines and bake at 180°C for about half an hour.
- Test if the food is ready by piercing the aubergines with a fork. If necessary, bake for a while longer.

Imam bayildi is a summer dish cooked all over the eastern Mediterranean.

LAMB *fricassee*

for 5-6 people

Ingredients

- *1-2 kg lamb shoulder, cut into portions*
- *1 kg endives, well washed*
- *10 spring onions, finely chopped*
- *1 large onion, grated on the grater*
- *1 cup olive oil*
- *salt, pepper*

for the avgolemono (egg-lemon) sauce

- *2 eggs*
- *1 cup dill, finely chopped*
- *juice of 1½ lemons*
- *salt, pepper*

- Heat the olive oil in a large saucepan and sauté the meat on all sides until golden brown.
- Remove the meat and add the spring onions and grated onion. Sauté until glossy.
- Put the meat back in, top up with 2 cups of hot water and cook for about 45 minutes.
- Add the endives into the pot, cover and cook for at least half an hour.
- Remove the pot from the heat and let the food cool slightly.
- Beat the egg whites in a bowl until they become a firm meringue.
- Beat the egg yolks well and add them gradually to the meringue, alternately with the lemon juice, stirring gently. At the end, add two ladles of broth from the pot, season with salt and pepper and add the chopped dill.
- Stir, and then pour the egg-lemon sauce into the pot with the meat.
- Gently shake the pot, holding by the handles, and put it back on the heat to bring to a boil for 1 or 2 minutes.
- Serve the food hot.

Avgolemono sauce is Greek and is not found in any other national cuisine. It takes a lot of skill to incorporate the egg with the rest of the ingredients without curdling the sauce.

SKEWERS
marinated with grape juice

for 4-5 people

Ingredients
- *2 tenderloins, of total weight 700 g*
- *6 sprigs of rosemary*
- *½ kg white grapes*
- *2 tablespoons dried oregano*
- *salt, pepper*

- Cut the tenderloins into pieces suitable for putting on skewers.
- Remove the leaves from the rosemary twigs, except for the little tuft on their ends. Use the rosemary sprigs as skewers for the meat.
- Put the skewers in a deep bowl. Season with salt and pepper and sprinkle with oregano.
- Put the grapes in a colander and place a bowl underneath. Crush the grapes with your hands and pour their juice over the skewers. Leave them in the refrigerator to marinate for 2-3 hours.
- Bake the skewers in a preheated oven at 200°C with the grill on, for about 20-30 minutes, until golden brown.
- Serve the skewers on the plates, and accompany with a fragrant potato salad.

Alternatively, you can put the pieces of meat on the special skewers.
You can also use chicken breast meat for this recipe.

MOUSSAKA

for 1 baking pan

Ingredients

- *6 globe aubergines*
- *oil for frying*
- *700g minced beef*
- *1 large onion, grated on the grater*
- *1 cup white wine*
- *¼ cup olive oil*
- *1 tablespoon tomato paste*
- *1 bay leaf*
- *1 pinch of cinnamon*
- *4 whole allspice grains*
- *salt, pepper*

for the béchamel sauce

- *4 tablespoons fresh butter*
- *4 tablespoons flour*
- *1-2 litres milk*
- *2 eggs*
- *1 pinch nutmeg*
- *1 cup Kasseri cheese, finely grated*
- *salt, white pepper*

- Remove the stems from the aubergines and slice into 1 cm-thick rounds. Salt them and let them sit in a colander for about ½ hour, to draw out any bitterness.
- Rinse with plenty of water and squeeze them. Pat them dry and fry into plenty of oil until golden brown. Place them on absorbent paper to drain the oil.
- Prepare the minced meat: In a large frying pan, heat the olive oil and sauté the onion until glossy. Add the minced meat and stir well. Deglaze the pan with the wine and cook until the alcohol evaporates.
- Dissolve the tomato paste in some water and pour it into the minced meat. Add the bay leaf, cinnamon, allspice, salt and pepper. Stir and cook over medium heat until the sauce thickens.
- Prepare the béchamel sauce: In a saucepan, melt the butter and add the flour. Stir with a whisk and lower the heat.
- Add the milk gradually, stirring constantly until the mixture thickens into a cream. Season with salt and pepper and add the nutmeg.
- Remove the pot from the heat, add the eggs, lightly beaten, stirring briskly and add the rest of the cheese into the béchamel sauce.
- Take a baking pan and place a layer of aubergines on the bottom, closely together leaving no gaps. Spread the minced meat over them in an even layer, and make a second layer with the remaining aubergines.
- Spread the béchamel sauce evenly on top and bake in a preheated oven at 170°C for about 1 hour, until golden brown.
- Allow to cool for ½ hour and serve.

For a lighter result, you can roast the aubergines in the oven until they are golden brown, after brushing their surface with a little olive oil. You can also add zucchini to the recipe.

MEATBALLS *with sauce*

for 4-5 people

Ingredients

- *400 g minced beef*
- *400 g minced pork*
- *1 onion, finely chopped in the food processor*
- *2 tablespoons spearmint, finely chopped*
- *200 g parmesan, finely grated*
- *salt, pepper*

for the sauce

- *½ kg fresh tomato juice*
- *¼ cup olive oil*
- *1 medium onion grated on the grater*
- *½ teaspoon cinnamon*
- *1 teaspoon sweet paprika*
- *1 tablespoon tomato paste*
- *salt, pepper*

- Place the two minced meats in a bowl together with the onion and knead well. Add the spearmint, parmesan, plenty of pepper and continue kneading until the mixture is well blended. Refrigerate for at least 1 hour.
- Prepare the sauce: In a large saucepan, heat the olive oil and sauté the onion until glossy. Add the tomato juice and the tomato paste. Stir until dissolved and let the sauce simmer for about 10 minutes. Add the cinnamon and paprika, season with salt and pepper.
- Remove the minced meat from the refrigerator and shape into balls the size of a small walnut. Add them to the pot with the sauce, shake it holding by the handles, half-cover it and simmer for at least half an hour until the meatballs are cooked through.
- Serve the food hot and accompany with white rice.

AUBERGINES *papoutsakia*

for 4 people

Ingredients

- *3 globe aubergines, medium*
- *½ kg minced beef*
- *1 large onion, grated*
- *4 tablespoons parsley, finely chopped*
- *2 cups fresh tomatoes, skin removed and grated (or canned coarsely cut tomato)*
- *olive oil*
- *salt, pepper*

for the béchamel sauce

- *4 tablespoons flour*
- *4 tablespoons butter*
- *1-2 litres of milk*
- *1 cup grated Kefalotyri cheese*
- *2 eggs*
- *salt, pepper*

- Remove the stems from the aubergines and cut them in half lengthwise. Salt them and let them sit in a colander for about half an hour, to draw out any bitterness. Pat them dry and fry in plenty of hot olive oil until they soften slightly. Place them on absorbent paper to drain the oil.
- Prepare the minced meat: In a large frying pan, heat the olive oil and sauté the onion until glossy. Add the minced meat and stir well.
- Add the tomatoes, season with salt and pepper and cook for about 20-25 minutes over medium heat until the sauce thickens. Remove from heat and add the parsley.
- Prepare the béchamel sauce: In a saucepan, melt the butter and add the flour. Stir with a whisk and lower the heat.
- Add the milk gradually, stirring constantly until the mixture thickens into a cream. Season with salt and pepper and add the nutmeg.
- Remove the pot from the heat, add the eggs, lightly beaten, half of the cheese and stir to incorporate all the ingredients.
- Spread the aubergines in an oven-proof dish and fill them with the minced meat.
- Put a spoonful of béchamel sauce over each aubergine, spread it evenly and sprinkle with the rest of the cheese.
- Bake in a preheated oven at 180°C for about 45 minutes, until golden brown.

You can serve the 'papoutsakia' over tomato sauce.

STUFFED *zucchini*

for 6-8 people

Ingredients

- *1½ kg medium zucchini*
- *500 g minced beef*
- *½ cup medium-grain white 'carolina' rice*
- *½ cup olive oil*
- *1 medium grated onion*
- *1 grated tomato*
- *2 tablespoons parsley, finely chopped*
- *5-6 leaves spearmint, finely chopped*
- *salt, pepper*

for the avgolemono (egg-lemon) sauce

- *2 eggs*
- *juice of 2 lemons*
- *salt, pepper*

- Wash and peel the zucchini, cut the ends off and keep one of the two (it will serve as a lid).
- With the special coring tool or a teaspoon remove the flesh from the zucchini and grate some of it.
- Put the minced meat, onion, rice, grated zucchini flesh, tomato and herbs in a bowl.
- Season with salt and pepper, add 2 tablespoons olive oil and mix well.
- With a teaspoon, stuff the zucchini, close them with the lids you kept and place them upright in a wide and shallow pot.
- Drizzle with the rest of the oil, salt, add 2 cups of water and let the food simmer over medium heat for about 45 minutes, regularly checking if you need to add more water.
- Remove the pot from the heat and let the food cool slightly.
- Prepare the egg-lemon sause: Beat the egg whites in a bowl until they become a firm meringue.
- Beat the egg yolks well and add them gradually to the meringue, alternately with the lemon juice, stirring gently. At the end, slowly add 2 ladles of broth from the pot and a little salt and pepper.
- Pour the egg-lemon sauce over the zucchini, shake the pot gently and put it back on the heat to come to a boil.

This mixture can be used also to fill tomatoes and peppers.

STUFFED *vegetables*

for 4 people

Ingredients

- *4 large red and firm tomatoes*
- *4 green peppers*
- *10 tablespoons medium-grain white 'carolina' rice*
- *3 large onions, finely chopped*
- *1 bunch parsley, finely chopped*
- *1 cup spearmint, finely chopped*
- *1½ cups olive oil*
- *1 tablespoon tomato paste, dissolved in a cup water*
- *¼ cup black seedless raisins*
- *¼ cup pine nuts*
- *1 cup breadcrumbs*
- *2 tablespoons sugar*
- *salt, pepper*

⊙ Cut one slice (lid) of each tomatos carefully scoop out the flesh with a spoon and finely chop it.

⊙ Cut one slice (lid) of each pepper and carefully remove the seeds.

⊙ In a deep frying pan heat the olive oil and sauté the onion until glossy. Add the rice and continue sautéing until the liquids are somewhat absorbed. Add the flesh of the tomatoes and the tomato paste.

⊙ As soon as the mixture comes to a boil, add the raisins, pine nuts and herbs. Season with salt and pepper, add the sugar and stir. Let the mixture simmer for 5 minutes and remove from the heat.

⊙ Fill the empty tomatoes and the peppers up to three quarters. Put on the lids. Drizzle a little oil over them and sprinkle with breadcrumbs.

⊙ Bake in a preheated oven at 200°C for about 1 hour.

⊙ Serve and accompany with Feta cheese or Greek yoghurt.

If you like, you can also stuff zucchini and aubergines.

STIFADO

for 6 people

Ingredients

- *1½ kg rump steak, cut into portions*
- *1 kg shallots*
- *1 large onion, grated on the grater*
- *4 garlic cloves, finely chopped*
- *3 bay leaves*
- *1 stick of cinnamon*
- *1 cup olive oil*
- *2 cups sweet wine*
- *1 shot cognac*
- *1 cup tomato juice*
- *salt, pepper*

- Peel and thoroughly wash the shallots.
- Heat the olive oil in a large pot and sauté the shallots for 5 minutes. Remove them from the pot, add the meat and sauté.
- Add the grated onion, garlic and continue to sauté for 2-3 minutes.
- Add the sweet wine and 1 cup of water and cook over medium heat for about 1 hour.
- Add the spring onions, bay leaves, cinnamon and pepper into the pot. Add the rest of the wine and cognac. Season with salt and pepper and cook over medium heat for about half an hour.
- Add the tomato juice and continue cooking for another 15-20 minutes, until the sauce thickens.

The traditional stifado is made with rabbit or hare.

The stew is named after the ancient Greek word "typhos", which means "steam".

PASTITSIO

for 8 people

Ingredients

- *600 g minced beef*
- *1 onion, finely chopped*
- *4 tablespoons olive oil*
- *400 g grated ripe tomatoes*
- *1 tablespoon sweet paprika*
- *1 teaspoon cinnamon*
- *½ kg thick pasta for pastitsio (like bucatini, ziti, rigatoni)*
- *½ cup fresh butter*
- *2 cups grated cheese*
- *salt, pepper*

for the béchamel sauce

- *4 tablespoons butter*
- *4 tablespoons flour*
- *1-2 litres of milk*
- *2 eggs*
- *salt, white pepper*
- *a few pinches of nutmeg, grated*

- In a saucepan, heat the olive oil and sauté the onion and minced meat, stirring constantly.
- Add the paprika and cinnamon. Season with salt and pepper and add the grated tomatoes.
- Simmer for about 30 minutes until the sauce thickens.
- Meanwhile, boil the pasta in plenty of salted water.
- Strain and sprinkle with half the amount of cheese.
- Prepare the béchamel sauce: In a saucepan, melt the butter and add the flour. Stir with a whisk and lower the heat.
- Add the milk gradually, stirring constantly until the mixture thickens into a cream.
- Season with salt and pepper and add the nutmeg.
- Remove the pot from the heat, add the eggs, lightly beaten, stir vigorously and add the rest of the cheese.
- Layer half of the pasta in a lightly buttered oven-proof dish.
- Layer the minced meat on top and finish with the rest of the pasta.
- Spread the béchamel sauce evenly and sprinkle some cheese on it.
- Bake in a preheated oven at 170°C for about 45 minutes until the surface turns golden brown.
- Allow to cool for a bit and serve.

SOUTZOUKAKIA *smyrneika*

for 6-8 people

Ingredients
- *1 kg minced beef*
- *2-3 garlic cloves, crushed*
- *1 tablespoon ground cumin*
- *200 g stale bread, soaked in red wine*
- *oil for frying*
- *salt, pepper*

for the sauce
- *1 onion, grated*
- *1 garlic clove, crushed*
- *¼ cup olive oil*
- *3 cups tomato juice*
- *½ cup water*
- *1 levelled tablespoon cumin*
- *salt, pepper*
- *optionally, 1 handful green olives*

- Squeeze the soaked bread, crumble it and put it in a basin.
- Add the minced meat, garlic, cumin and season with salt and pepper.
- Knead well and let the mixture rest for 1-2 hours in the refrigerator.
- Prepare the tomato sauce: Heat the olive oil in a saucepan and sauté the onion and garlic until glossy.
- Add the tomato juice and water and bring to a boil. Add the cumin, salt and pepper.
- While the sauce is boiling, shape the minced meat into oblong meatballs.
- Fry them over medium to high heat, without flouring them, until they brown.
- Place the soutzoukakia in the simmering sauce and cook for about half an hour.
- If desired, add a handful of green olives into the pot 2-3 minutes before turning off the heat.
- Serve with boiled seasonal vegetables and rice.

If you want a lighter result, you can use sunflower oil instead of olive oil when frying.

CHICKEN SOUP *with avgolemono*

for 4-5 people

Ingredients

- *1 chicken about 1½ kg*
- *1 whole onion, peeled*
- *3 sprigs of celery*
- *2 carrots*
- *200 g of 'carolina' rice*

for the avgolemono (egg-lemon) sauce

- *2 eggs*
- *juice of 2 lemons*
- *salt, pepper*

Chicken soup is the very definition of comfort food. Every home cook in Greece prepares it when a member of the family is sick with the flu or a cold.

- Wash the chicken well and place it in a pot with the onion, celery, carrots and salt. Cover with water and boil for at least 1 hour.
- Taste if the chicken is well-cooked and remove from the pot along with the vegetables.
- Add the rice to the boiling broth after you have rinsed it thoroughly with cold water, and stir well. Taste, add a little salt if needed and let the rice cook.
- Prepare the avgolemono: Separate the egg whites from the yolks. Beat the egg whites into a meringue. Beat the yolks until they turn pale white. Combine the two ingredients, mixing gently and add the lemon juice. At the end, slowly add 2 ladles of broth from the pot and a little salt and pepper.
- Pour the avgolemono into the soup, shake the pot gently and put it back on the heat to come to a boil.

If you want, you can debone the chicken, cut the meat into small pieces and add it to the soup. Otherwise, cut it into portions and serve on a platter.

FISH SOUP

for 4-5 people

Ingredients

- *1½ kg of fish (scorpionfish, dusky grouper, sea bream, white grouper)*
- *4 medium potatoes*
- *3 carrots*
- *5 sprigs of celery*
- *1 whole tomato*
- *2 whole onions*
- *salt, pepper*
- *juice of 2 lemons*

- Peel the vegetables, wash them well, place them in a large pot, and add water to cover them.
- Cook for 45-50 minutes until the potatoes are well softened.
- In the last 10 minutes add the fish.
- Once the fish are cooked, remove them with a slotted spoon, allow to cool and carefully divide the fish into large pieces.
- Add salt and pepper to the pot and use a hand blender to mash the vegetables until you have a nice velvety soup.
- Add the lemon juice and stir gently.
- Serve in deep soup dishes, adding pieces of fish.

Kakavia is the oldest Greek fish soup, named after the word "kakavi", a three-legged cooking vessel used by ancient Ionian fishermen.

SHRIMP *saganaki*

for 2 people

Ingredients

- *12 large shrimp*
- *2 onions, sliced into rounds*
- *1 green pepper, finely chopped*
- *1 garlic clove, finely chopped*
- *1 bowl fresh tomato, grated*
- *2 teaspoons tomato paste*
- *200 g Feta cheese*
- *1 cup olive oil*
- *salt, pepper*

- Put water to boil in a pot, add some salt, add the shrimp and let boil for 2-3 minutes.
- Take the shrimp out of the pot and place them on a plate, saving the broth. Shell the shrimp.
- In another saucepan, heat some olive oil and sauté the onion, pepper and garlic until glossy.
- Add the fresh tomato, stir and season with salt and pepper. Add some of the broth in which the shrimp boiled.
- Wait for them to come to a boil, add the tomato paste and sprinkle with a bit of salt. Stir until the sauce thickens and turn off the heat.
- Take 2 small oven-proof dishes and place 6 shrimp on their bottom. Crumble the Feta cheese on top and cover with the sauce.
- Place the dishes in a preheated oven at 180°C for 3-4 minutes, to gratinate.

GALAKTOBOUREKO

for 1 baking pan

Ingredients
- *1 package phyllo pastry*
- *200 g fresh melted butter, for spreading on the phyllo*

for the cream
- *2 litres fresh milk*
- *400 g granulated sugar*
- *zest of 3 lemons*
- *240 g fine semolina*
- *90 g cornstarch*
- *100 g fresh butter*

for the syrup
- *2 cups sugar*
- *2 cups water*
- *peel of 1 lemon*

Syrup
- Put the water, sugar and lemon peel in a pot. Boil until it begins to thicken, remove from heat and let it cool down.

Cream
- Heat the milk in a large pot and add the sugar, lemon zest, semolina and the cornstarch dissolved in a little cold water.
- Stir constantly with gentle movements, raising the temperature, until the cream begins to thicken.
- Remove from heat, add the fresh butter and stir until melted.

Assembly
- Butter a rectangular baking pan and spread 4 phyllo sheets on the bottom, brushing them one by one with the fresh butter, making sure that each sheet protrudes from a different side of the pan.
- Stir the cream, pour it into the baking pan, spread evenly and fold the edges of the phyllo sheets inwards, brushing them with butter.
- Place another 4-5 sheets over the cream, buttering them one by one and cutting them to the dimensions of the pan so that they do not protrude.
- With a sharp knife, carve the top sheets of the galaktoboureko into portions.
- Place the baking pan in a preheated oven and bake at 170°C in the conventional oven setting (no fan) for about 45 minutes, until the phyllo pastry turns golden brown.
- Take the galaktoboureko out of the oven and slowly pour the cold syrup over it, with a ladle.
- Let the dessert absorb the syrup for about 20 minutes and serve in portions.

KATAIFI

for 1 baking pan

Ingredients

- *1 package kataifi pastry*
- *500 g ground walnuts*
- *1 teaspoon ground cinnamon*
- *1 teaspoon ground cloves*
- *250 g fresh butter*

for the syrup

- *2 cups sugar*
- *1 cup water*

- Put the walnuts, cinnamon and cloves in a bowl and mix.
- Take some of the kataifi pastry, shape into a 10x10 cm square, ½ cm thick, place a heaping spoonful of filling on its one end, wrap the kataifi piece into a roll and place it in a baking pan. Continue this same process until the pan is full.
- Melt the fresh butter in a saucepan and pour over the dessert.
- Bake in a preheated oven at 170°C for about 30 minutes, until the surface is golden brown.
- In the meantime, prepare the syrup: Put the water with the sugar in a pot and let it come to a boil. Keep it warm.
- Remove the kataifi from the oven and pour the hot syrup over it.
- Let it absorb the syrup for 10 minutes and serve.

Kataifi has its roots in the depths of Asia Minor and is made with a special shredded pastry that looks like fibers.

GREEK *baklava*

for 1 baking pan

Ingredients

- *1 package phyllo pastry*
- *1 kg walnuts, finely chopped*
- *1 cup sugar*
- *1 tablespoon ground cinnamon*
- *6-7 ground cloves*
- *220 g olive oil*
- *220 g thyme honey*

- Put the walnuts, sugar, cinnamon and cloves into a large bowl and mix well.
- Take a medium baking pan and lay a phyllo sheet on its bottom. Sprinkle it with 2-3 tablespoons of the walnut mixture.
- Repeat the procedure until the walnut mixture and sheets are finished, alternately layering them.
- With a very sharp knife, cut the baklava diagonally into portions, making sure to cut all the way to bottom of the baking pan.
- In a small pot, heat the olive oil until it starts to smoke.
- With a tablespoon, pour the hot oil over the baklava, mainly in the places where you cut through it.
- Bake in a preheated oven at 180°C for about 40-50 minutes, until the phyllo sheets are golden brown.
- Remove the baklava from the oven and while hot, pour the honey over, after heating it, again in the places where you have cut it, and let it absorb the honey for at least 15 minutes.
- Cut into portions and serve on a platter.

SEMOLINA *Halva*

for 6-8people

Ingredients

- *1 cup olive oil*
- *2 cups coarse semolina*

for the syrup

- *2 cups sugar*
- *¾ cup honey*
- *4 cups water*
- *1 orange (peel and juice)*
- *2 cinnamon sticks*
- *About 15 cloves*

- With a small knife, cut a strip of peel around the orange.
- In a small saucepan, boil the water for 5 minutes with the orange peel, cinnamon sticks, cloves, honey and sugar.
- Remove from heat, remove the peel, cinnamon sticks and cloves and set aside.
- In a pot, heat the oil until very hot, add the semolina and stir constantly until lightly roasted.
- Pour in the syrup gradually, stirring continuously. Add the juice of half an orange and stir constantly until the mixture has absorbed all the liquids and begins to come off the walls of the pot.
- Remove from heat and transfer the hot mixture into a mould.
- When it cools, unmould on a platter and garnish with the cloves, cinnamon and orange peel that you set aside.

You can let your imagination run wild with halva and add any ingredients you want, from dried fruit to chocolate.

GRAPE *spoon dessert*

for 2 jar

Ingredients
- *1 kg of seedless white grapes*
- *3 cups sugar*
- *4 cups water*
- *1 pinch of vanilla*
- *100 g blanched almonds*
- *juice of ½ lemon*

- Put the sugar with 4 cups of water and the vanilla in a pot and boil for about 10 minutes.
- Add the grapes, stir carefully to prevent the berries from breaking and continue boiling for about 15-20 minutes.
- Remove from the heat, cover the pot with a towel and leave it like this overnight.
- The next day boil again for 15 more minutes until the syrup thickens.
- Remove from heat, add the almonds, lemon juice and stir gently.
- Allow the sweet to cool off, put in sterilized jars and store them in the refrigerator.

If you want to keep the spoon sweet outside the fridge, after putting it in the jars, boil them for about 15 minutes.

Spoon sweets are made from nearly all fresh fruits and vegetables and in Greece they are synonymous with hospitality and welcoming visitors.

RECIPES from CRETE

⊙ ⊙ ⊙

Crete is the largest island in Greece. It was here that the Minoan civilization, considered the first in Europe, flourished thousands of years ago. Its residents are renowned for their hospitality and cuisine!

Since ancient times, it has been a self-sufficient island, able to produce nearly all basic goods and meet the needs of its inhabitants.

Olive oil is the central component of the Cretan diet. Moreover, Crete is home to the world's oldest olive tree. It is over 3,000 years old, yet it continues to bear fruit!

The entire island is dotted with olive trees, and their olive oil is regarded as among the finest in the world. That is why butter is rarely used in Cretan recipes.

In the mountains of Crete we find numerous herds of goats and sheep, whose meat is extraordinarily flavorful due to their diet of wild greens and the precious herbs of the Cretan land, and whose milk yields cheeses such as graviera and anthotyro, which are renowned for their exquisite flavor around the globe.

The Cretan rusk is also well-known, particularly the barley rusk, a staple of the Cretan diet.

However, Crete is also renowned for its wine, with excellent wines to show, primarily using local varieties such as *Mandilari* and *Vilana*, as well as its raki, a strong drink that is almost always offered in restaurants and taverns.

So to your health, and enjoy!

SUMMER SALAD
with amaranth greens, zucchini, potatoes and tomatoes

for 6 people

Ingredients
- *½ kg zucchini*
- *600 g peeled potatoes*
- *500 g amaranth greens*
- *2 large ripe tomatoes*
- *olive oil*
- *vinegar or lemon*
- *salt*

- Put 3 litres of water in a large pot with a little salt and, as soon as it comes to a boil, put in the potatoes.
- Boil for around 20 minutes and add the zucchini.
After 5 minutes add the amaranth greens. Add the 2 tomatoes and continue boiling for about 15 minutes.
- Remove from heat and remove the tomatoes.
- Place all the potatoes together on a large platter, and the zucchini next to them, and then cut them. Then put the amaranth greens.
- Place the tomatoes on top and crush them with a fork, for their juice to cover the vegetables.
- Drizzle with plenty of olive oil, a little vinegar or lemon, at taste, and coarse salt.
- Serve with fresh bread and black olives.

If you like, you can omit the tomatoes. The salad will be just as flavorful.

Every summer, amaranth greens have their place on the Greek table. They make an extremely tasty and nutritious salad.

CRETAN *dakos*

for 4 people

Ingredients
- *4 barley rusks*
- *600 g ripe tomatoes, grated*
- *1 cup fine olive oil*
- *300 g Cretan Xinomizithra cheese or Feta cheese*
- *20 black salt-cured olives (throumbes)*
- *oregano, fresh or dried*

- On a large platter, place the barley rusks, drizzle them with a little water and with half the olive oil.
- Spread the grated tomatoes over the dakos rusks. Any tomatoes left over, place them around the rusks.
- Put the Xinomizithra cheese or coarsely grated Feta cheese on top.
- Sprinkle with plenty of oregano, garnish with the olives and pour the rest of the olive oil over the dakos.

You can also make dakos with any other rusk of your choice.

Barley rusks were and are very widespread in the diet of the Cretans. Nowadays you can find them in all supermarkets.

KALTSOUNAKIA

for 25 pieces

Ingredients

for the dough

- *5 cups all-purpose flour*
- *1¼ cup water*
- *2 tablespoons ouzo or raki*
- *¼ cup olive oil*
- *½ teaspoon salt*

for the filling

- *½ kg fresh Mizithra cheese*
- *3 tablespoons spearmint, finely chopped*
- *2 eggs*

- *oil for frying*
- *sesame seeds for sprinkling*
- *honey for serving*

- Mix the flour with the salt in a bowl and open a hole in the centre. Add the water, oil, ouzo and stir until it becomes a soft dough.
- Sprinkle the countertop with flour, transfer the dough and continue kneading, adding as much flour as needed to get a smooth and supple dough. Put it in a bowl, cover and let it rest for a least ½ hour.
- In the meantime, prepare the stuffing: Put the Mizithra cheese, eggs and spearmint in a bowl and mix until it becomes a homogeneous mixture.
- Divide the dough into balls and roll out 10 cm disks with a rolling pin.
- Put 1 tablespoon of the mixture on the half side of each disk, fold the other half over it so as to form a crescent, and press the edges with a fork to seal well.
- Repeat the process until all the dough is finished.
- In a frying pan, heat the olive oil and fry the 'kaltsounakia' on both sides until golden brown.
- While still hot, sprinkle with sesame seeds, pour the honey over them and serve.

SQUID (calamari) in wine sauce with green olives and fennel

for 4-5 people

Ingredients

- *1 kg squid, well cleaned and cut into large pieces*
- *¼ cup olive oil*
- *2 large onions, grated on a grater*
- *1 cup dry white wine*
- *20 pitted green olives*
- *1 cup fennel, finely chopped*
- *juice of 1 lemon*
- *salt, pepper*

- Heat the olive oil in a pot and sauté the squid along with the onions until glossy.
- Pour in the white wine, stir and when it evaporates add 1 cup of water.
- Cover the pot and cook over medium heat for about ¾ of an hour.
- Add the green olives, season with salt and pepper and continue cooking for about 15 minutes until the sauce thickens.
- Add the lemon juice, stir, add the fennel and simmer for about 15 minutes. If needed add a little water.
- Serve the food hot.

In excavations at the palace of Knossos, edible olives have been found, while there are also ideograms depicting the blessed fruit of the olive tree.

LAMB *stew with fennel*

for 6 people

Ingredients

- *1½ kg leg of lamb cut into portions*
- *½ kg fresh fennel*
- *6 spring onions, finely chopped*
- *juice of 2 lemons*
- *1 cup olive oil*
- *2 tablespoons tomato paste*
- *salt, pepper*

- Wash the fennel well and finely chop it.
- Heat the olive oil in a large pot and sauté the meat with the spring onions. Season with salt and pepper and add the fennel and the tomato paste dissolved in 2 cups of water
- Bring the food to a good boil and lower the heat. Cook for about 1 hour until the sauce thickens and the meat becomes tender. If necessary, add a little water.
- Add the lemon juice, bring the food to a boil and remove the pot from the heat.

Fennel is a herb known since ancient times for its beneficial properties.

HOHLIOI *Boubouristoi (snails savoro)*

for 6 people

Ingredients

- *1½ kg of scalded snails*
- *1 cup olive oil*
- *3 garlic cloves, finely chopped*
- *¼ cup fresh rosemary leaves*
- *2 tablespoons flour*
- *¼ cup red wine vinegar*
- *pepper*
- *coarse salt for seasoning*

- In a large frying pan, heat the olive oil well and add the garlic. Immediately add the snails and stir constantly until they are covered with oil.
- Add the rosemary and the flour and continue stirring.
- Add pepper, cook over low heat for a few minutes and deglaze with the vinegar.
- Serve in a deep platter and sprinkle with coarse salt.

To remove the cooked snail from the shell, first you need to slightly crack the centre of the shell. Then, using the special fork, pierce the snail and turn it in a circular motion until you pull it all out.

Another name for rosemary herb is the "rose of Mary". According to legend, the Virgin Mary left her cloak on a bush, which the next morning was full of small blue fragrant flowers.

LYCHNARAKIA

for 25 pieces

Ingredients

for the dough

- 2 teaspoons fresh yeast
or 1 sachet of dry yeast
- 4 tablespoons milk
- 4 cups flour
- ½ cup oil
- 2/3 cup sugar
- 2 eggs, beaten with a little salt
- 3 tablespoons Greek yoghurt

for the filling

- 4 cups unsalted Mizithra cheese
- 2 egg yolks
- 1 pinch of vanilla
- 2 tablespoons honey
- 2 tablespoons lemon zest
- 2 tablespoons cinnamon
- 2 tablespoons unsalted butter
- 6 tablespoons sugar
- 1 egg yolk beaten with a little water
- salt

- Dissolve the yeast in the milk, add 1 teaspoon of flour and leave the mixture in a warm place until it rises. (If you use instant yeast, you just add it into the flour.)
- In a deep bowl, whisk the oil and sugar into a creamy mixture. Add the eggs, yoghurt, salt and the flour mixture that has risen. Stir well and slowly add the rest of the flour.
- Transfer the mixture to a floured surface and knead until a smooth and soft dough is formed, which won't stick to the hands. Cover the dough and let it rest for half an hour.
- In a bowl, crush the Mizithra cheese with a fork, add the yolks, vanilla, honey, lemon zest, half the cinnamon, butter, sugar and mix well, until the mixture is homogeneous.
- Roll the dough into a sheet, about half a centimetre thick, and cut round disks with the help of a cup.
- Place a tablespoon of filling in the centre of each disk and with your fingers pinch the dough all around, creating 8-10 small 'peaks'.
- Brush the surface with egg and sprinkle with the remaining cinnamon.
- Butter a baking pan and place the 'lychnarakia' inside.
- Bake in a preheated oven at 180°C for about half an hour or until golden brown.

Lychnarakia was a favourite Easter dessert, but now you can find it at all times of the year.

RECIPES from CYCLADES ISLANDS

In the heart of the Aegean Sea lie the Cyclades islands, a cluster of 56 small and large islands that are permeated with the aroma and scents of the sea and herbs.

Their beauties are abundant, and so are their delicacies. These islands are composed of stone, salt, and wind. Stone was used by the inhabitants to form terraces on the slopes to grow vegetables, which the wind and the salt, combined with the scant rainfall, give a unique taste. A typical example are the tomatoes and white eggplants of Santorini.

As they are mostly semi-mountainous islands, their inhabitants run small-scale livestock farms, which produce extremely flavorful cheeses. The varieties, which exceed 25, vary from place to place and some of them have been declared as Protected Designation of Origin. The top Cycladic cheeses are considered to be the *kopanisti* from Mykonos, a cream cheese with intense flavor, *San Michali* from Syros, which resembles Parmesan, and the spicy *Arseniko* from Naxos.

Of course, fish and seafood could not be absent from the Cycladic diet, cooked with flair and imagination. Octopus balls and cod fritters, prepared with herbs and love, prawn pilaf, and an abundance of other delectable flavors make the Cyclades a great gastronomic destination that will not disappoint any palate!

SALAD *with cherry tomatoes, caper leaves and Anthotyro cheese*

for 1 salad bowl

Ingredients

- *600 g cherry tomatoes*
- *200 g fresh Anthotyro cheese or ricotta cheese*
- *20 pickled caper leaves*
- *2 tablespoons balsamic vinegar*
- *olive oil*
- *salt*

- Wash the cherry tomatoes well, let them dry and cut them in half with a knife.
- Grate the Anthotyro cheese on the coarse side of the grater.
- Rinse the caper leaves with plenty of cold water and let them dry.
- Put the cherry tomatoes in a salad bowl, salt them, add plenty of olive oil, vinegar and mix very well. Add the caper leaves around the salad bowl, to rest on its walls. In the middle, place the grated Anthotyro cheese.

If you don't serve your salad right away, refrigerate it.

Capers: A plant with beautiful flowers. An herb rich in vitamins. A pickle with a unique flavor.

BAKED *chickpeas*

for 4-6 people

Ingredients

- *1 kg chickpeas*
- *2 large onions, coarsely chopped*
- *1 cup olive oil*
- *salt, pepper*
- *3 tablespoons flour*

- Soak the chickpeas in water overnight. The next day, rub them between your hands to remove the skins, wash well and boil in plenty salted water until soft.
- Put the chickpeas in a clay oven-proof dish, add the onion, olive oil, salt, pepper, and 3 tablespoons of flour dissolved in a cup of water.
- Add water to cover the chickpeas, cover the dish and bake in a preheated oven at 180°C for about an hour.

Sifnos has a long tradition in gastronomy, as it was the birthplace of the great Greek cook of the 20th century, Nikos Tselementes.

FOURTALIA

for 1 large frying pan

Ingredients

- *½ kg potatoes, peeled and cut into cubes*
- *200 g country-style sausage, cut into thin slices*
- *6 eggs*
- *2 tablespoons butter*
- *olive oil*
- *salt, pepper*

- Put plenty of olive oil in a frying pan and fry the potatoes.
- In another pan, sauté the sausage.
- In a large clean frying pan, put 2 tablespoons of butter, add the fried potatoes, cooked sausage and stir to spread over the entire surface of the pan.
- Beat the eggs in a bowl, season with salt and pepper and pour them over the potatoes and sausages.
- Cook the omelette well on one side, turn it over with a lid, cook on the other side, and serve it hot.

Fourtalia is a traditional dish of Andros island. This is an omelette that always has some other ingredient in it, along with the eggs. It is usually potato cubes or Andros sausage but also various blanched greens, boiled broad beans, even small fried fish in the summer.

TRADITIONAL *fava*

for 4-5 people

Ingredients

- *½ kg of yellow split peas ('fava')*
- *salt*
- *1 cup olive oil*

for garnishing

- *1 onion cut into matchsticks*

- Wash the split peas well with plenty of cold water.
- Put in a saucepan and cover with water by about 4 centimeters higher than the peas.
- When it comes to a boil, remove the foam and stir constantly so that it does not stick. Add some hot water if necessary. Stirring must be continuous otherwise it can easily stick to the bottom of the pot.
- When the split peas start to break up and form a puree, remove the pot from the heat and let it cool.
- Use a hand blender to puree, add the olive oil, season with salt and continue blending until it turns into a velvety cream.
- Serve in a bowl, garnish with the onion cut into matchsticks and drizzle with a little olive oil.

Fava is a favorite dish across Greece. It comes from the 'lathouri' legume, which is rich in protein, carbohydrates and fibre. It is said that the best fava on the islands is produced in Santorini, where it is served with caramelised onion, which gives it great flavor and they call it "Married Fava".

TOMATO *fritters*

for 4-6 people

Ingredients

- *2-3 onions, finely chopped*
- *1 kg grated tomatoes*
- *1 cup fresh spearmint, finely chopped*
- *500 g self-rising flour (as much as needed)*
- *salt, pepper*
- *oil for frying*

- Put all the ingredients in a deep bowl, stir until a soft mixture is formed and leave in the refrigerator to rest for 1 hour.
- Heat plenty of oil in a deep frying pan. Drop spoonfuls of the mixture in the oil and fry on both sides, until golden brown.
- Put the fritters for a few minutes on absorbent paper, to drain the oil, and serve.

Santorini has not always been the cosmopolitan island it is today. The people of Santorini lived almost exclusively off the products they produced, the arid small tomatoes, capers, the unique white aubergines and fava. In Santorini you will go for the landscapes, the sea and the uniqueness of the Caldera, but you will stay for the food.

COD *fritters*

for 6 people

Ingredients

- *1 kg salted cod, well soaked to remove the salt*
- *1 onion, pulped in the food processor*
- *¼ cup spearmint, finely chopped*
- *¼ cup dill, finely chopped*
- *2 eggs*
- *salt, pepper*
- *flour, as much as needed*
- *olive oil for frying*
- *beer (if needed)*

- Remove the fins, bones and skin from the cod, cut into very small pieces with your hands, and put it in a large bowl.
- Add the onion, spear mint, dill, a little salt and pepper, and mix well.
- Sift the flour and add it gradually, stirring constantly until the mixture becomes a thick batter. If it becomes too thick, dilute with a little beer.
- Put the mixture in the refrigerator for 1 hour.
- Heat plenty of oil in a deep frying pan. Drop spoonfuls of the mixture in the oil and fry over medium heat on both sides until golden brown.
- Put the cod fritters for a few minutes on absorbent paper, to drain the oil, and serve with skordalia.

You can make fish fritters with any fresh fish of your choice.

OCTOPUS *fritters*

for 5-6 people

Ingredients

- *1 octopus, around 1 kg*
- *1 large onion, grated*
- *¼ cup spearmint, finely chopped*
- *150 g soft grated cheese*
- *1 egg*
- *all-purpose flour*
- *salt, pepper*
- *oil for frying*

- Clean the octopus well, remove the mouth and eyes, wash it, cut it into small pieces, put them in the blender and beat into a pulp.
- Pour the pulp into a bowl, add the onion, spearmint, cheese, egg, a little salt and pepper.
- Knead well to make the mixture homogeneous. Add flour and continue kneading until the mixture begins to thicken. Let it rest for 2 hours and knead again.
- Heat plenty of oil in a deep frying pan. Drop spoonfuls of the mixture in the oil and fry over medium heat on both sides until golden brown.
- Put the fritters for a few minutes on absorbent paper, to drain the oil, and serve.

On small islands where fishing was the primary occupation, housewives cooked fritters with a variety of seafood and garden herbs. Today these fritters are sought after for their simplicity and deliciousness.

SHRIMP *pilaf*

for 6 people

Ingredients

- *24 fresh medium shrimp*
- *1 cup rice*
- *¼ cup olive oil*
- *1 onion, grated*
- *1 cup canned coarsely cut tomatoes*
- *1 tablespoon tomato paste*
- *1 levelled tablespoon sugar*
- *1 tablespoon crushed dry coriander*
- *1 levelled tablespoon sweet paprika*
- *salt, pepper*

for the broth

- *1 small onion, cut in half*
- *1 carrot*
- *1 celery stalk*
- *1 cup white wine*
- *1 cup water*
- *the heads and the tails of the shrimp*

- Shell the shrimp, remove their intestine and cut off the tail and head.
- Place the tails and heads of the shrimp, onion, carrot, celery, wine and water in a large pot and boil over medium heat for abou ½ hour.
- Remove the pot from the heat, strain by pressing the ingredients well in a colander and keep the broth aside.
- Prepare the pilaf: Heat the olive oil in a large pot and sauté the onion until glossy.
- Add the rice, mix well with a wooden spoon until it absorbs all the oil and pour in the canned tomato. Dissolve the tomato paste in some water and add it to the pot.
- Add 1 cup of the broth you have set aside, mix well and bring the food to a boil. Add the sugar, paprika, coriander, salt and pepper.
- Stir and let simmer for 5 minutes. Add the shrimp, stir and continue cooking until the rice is cooked. If needed, add some water.
- Turn off the heat, let the pilaf absorb its liquids for 10 minutes and serve.

Shrimp is a favourite seafood across the Mediterranean countries. Greeks have included it in their diet since ancient times.

LAMB *with artichokes*

for 4-6 people

Ingredients

- *1½ kg lamb cut into portions*
- *12 artichokes, peeled and rubbed with lemon*
- *2 large onions, grated on a grater*
- *3 green onions, finely chopped*
- *¼ cup olive oil*

for the avgolemono (egg-lemon) sauce

- *3 eggs*
- *juice of 2 lemons*
- *salt, pepper*
- *1 cup dill, finely chopped*

- In a large pot, heat the olive oil and sauté the lamb until it is slightly browned. Take it out and place on a large plate.
- Add the green onions and artichokes to the pot and sauté them well.
- Add the meat, season with salt and pepper, add a little water and cook for about 1 hour.
- In the meantime prepare the avgolemono sauce: Beat the egg whites in a bowl until they become a firm meringue.
- Beat the egg yolks well and add them gratually to the meringue, alternating with the lemon juice, stirring gently. At the end slowly add 2 ladles of broth from the pot, the dill and season with salt and pepper.
- Stir and pour the sauce in the pot with the meat and artichokes.
- Shake the pot gently and put it back on the heat to bring to a boil for 1-2 minutes.
- Serve the food while hot.

When a man is open-hearted and kind, we say he has an artichoke heart. This means that his heart is soft and sensitive, like the plant's.

You can taste the artichokes raw with plenty of lemon and salt. It is an ideal snack for a tsipouro or ouzo.

KALOGIROS

for 4-6 people

Ingredients

- *1 kg beef chuck cut, into cubes*
- *1 large onion, grated on the grater*
- *2 garlic cloves, crushed*
- *2 cups tomato juice*
- *1 tablespoon tomato paste*
- *1 cup red wine*
- *¼ cup olive oil*
- *4 globe aubergines, cut into thick slices*
- *300 g coarsely grated Naxos Graviera cheese*
- *flour for coating*
- *olive oil for frying*
- *salt, pepper*

- Heat the olive oil in a deep pot and sauté the on all sides until well browned.
- Add the onion with the garlic and continue sautéing for 2-3 more minutes.
- Deglaze with the wine and when it evaporates, add the tomato juice, salt and pepper.
- As soon as the food starts to boil, lower the heat and simmer for about 1 hour, until the meat is tender.
- In the meantime, prepare the aubergines: Salt them and let them sit in a colander for about 15-30 minutes, to draw out any bitterness. Rinse them, squeeze well, salt and flour them.
- Fry the aubergines in hot olive oil on all sides until golden brown and place on absorbent paper to drain the excess oil.
- Serve in the following way: Put the aubergines on a platter, place the meat on top and sprinkle with the coarsely grated Graviera cheese.

This dish owes its name to the dark colour of aubergines, which resembles the robes worn by monks.

LADENIA

for 2-3 people

Ingredients

- *½ kg self-rising flour*
- *300 g lukewarm water*
- *⅓ cup olive oil*
- *2 tomatoes, skins removed and cut into cubes*
- *1 large onion, peeled and cut into matchsticks*
- *salt*
- *oregano*

- Sift the flour in a bowl and add the salt and the lukewarm water gradually. Knead the mixture until a soft dough is formed.
- Leave it to rest for ½ hour and knead again.
- Brush a round baking pan about 25 cm in diameter with plenty of oil. Place the dough in the centre of the baking pan and press it with your fingers until it covers the entire bottom of the baking pan.
- Spread the tomato and onion on the dough, sprinkle with oregano and drizzle with the rest of the olive oil.
- Lightly salt and bake the ladenia in a preheated oven at 180°C for 35-40 minutes.
- Let the food cool, cut in pieces and serve.

Ladenia is a simple but extremely tasty dish. It is considered the great-grandfather of pizza! Kimolos is its birthplace, but now it is made in all Cycladic islands.

Kimolos is a small, volcanic island. It takes its name from the Greek word for chalk, a rock that abounds in its subsoil.

LOLI

for 1 round pan

Ingredients

- *1 kg pumpkin, grated on the grater*
- *½ kg all-purpose flour*
- *1 cup orange juice*
- *1 gcup olive oil*
- *1 cup sugar*
- *¼ cup cognac*
- *1 teaspoon cinnamon*
- *½ teaspoon ground clove*
- *1 teaspoon baking powder (or baking soda)*
- *2 tablespoons honey*
- *zest of 2 oranges*
- *300 g black raisins*
- *sesame seeds*

- Put the flour and all the ingredients except for the pumpkin in a large bowl and mix well. Add the pumpkin and stir again.
- Spread the mixture on a buttered round 35cm baking pan and sprinkle with plenty of sesame seeds.
- Bake in a preheated oven at 180°C for about 1 hour.
- Let the pie cool, cut in pieces and serve.

If you prefer, you can use other seasonings, such as nutmeg, or add orange zest for even more intensity of flavor.

The yellow pumpkin is a vegetable that loves spices and herbs, and features in both sweet and savoury recipes.

RECIPES from PELOPONNESE

The Peloponnese is a blessed place, with its varied landscape, rich history, and distinctive products.

Olives, vines, fruit trees, or extremely rare cheeses... each region has its own specialties and native produce: Figs from Kalamata, raisins from Corinthia, cherries from Sparta, Tsakonian aubergines from Leonidio, and a variety of wines from Achaia, including the fine *Agiorgitiko*, aromatic *Moschofilero*, and sweet *Mavrodaphne*.

Special mention should be made to a very spicy Messinian cheese, *Sfela*, which is ideal for grilling. In the same area rovitsa, a rare green bean, is produced, which can be cooked as a puree or even soup.

Pure products and unique recipes, ideal for lovers of good food!

STRAPATSADA

for 5-6 people

Ingredients

- *6 eggs*
- *1 kg grated tomatoes*
- *1 green pepper, finely chopped*
- *¼ cup olive oil*
- *1 small onion, grated on a grater*
- *250 g Syglino cured pork, cut into small pieces*
- *salt, pepper*

- In a large frying pan, heat the olive oil and sauté the onion with the pepper until glossy.
- Add the grated tomatoes, some salt and pepper.
- As soon as the sauce starts to boil, lower the heat and cook until it thickens.
- Beat the eggs as you do for an omelette, add them into the pan and stir constantly with a wooden spoon to incorporate with the sauce.
- Add the Syglino, cook for 1 more minute and remove the pan from the heat.
- Serve the strapatsada on a platter and accompany with fried potatoes and dry red wine.

Syglino is a traditional Greek cured meat, consisting of pieces of pork which, after being well salted and seasoned with spices or herbs, are smoked and preserved in fat.

ZUCCHINI FLOWERS *stuffed with cheese*

for 5-6 people

Ingredients

- *20 fresh zucchini flowers*
- *200 g Kasseri cheese, cut into cubes*

for the batter

- *1½ cup flour*
- *1 sachet dry yeast*
- *salt*
- *olive oil for frying*

- Prepare the batter: In a bowl mix the flour with the yeast, gradually add lukewarm water, salt well and leave it in a cool place for 1 hour for the yeast to activate.
- Take the zucchini flowers one at a time, carefully remove the stamens and put 2-3 cubes of Kasseri cheese inside them.
- Turn the ends of the blossom petals inwards and lightly press them to secure them.
- Dip the zucchini blossoms into the batter and fry them in hot oil until they are golden brown and the cheese melts.
- Place them on absorbent paper for a few minutes to drain the oil and serve them hot and accompany with ouzo.

Zucchini flowers are not washed because they wither and spoil. If you want, you can grate the Kasseri cheese on the fine side of the grater and mix it with a beaten egg into a firm dough-like batter.

The orange-yellow blooms of zucchini are edible and can be prepared in a variety of ways, including stuffing with various ingredients and frying in batter.

SLIM AUBERGINES *with Feta cheese*

for 5-6 people

Ingredients

- *1½ kg aubergines*
- *olive oil for frying*
- *3 cups fresh tomatoes, finely chopped*
- *350 g Feta cheese, crumbled*
- *1 large onion, grated on the grater*
- *4 cloves garlic, finely chopped*
- *¼ cup spearmint, finely chopped*
- *4 tablespoons olive oil for the sauce and a little more for the frying*
- *salt, pepper*

- Wash the aubergines well, cut them lenghwise, salt well and put them in a colander for half an hour. Then rinse them well and squeeze them with your hands.
- Put plenty of olive oil in a pan and fry the aubergines until they are lightly browned. Place them on absorbent paper to drain the oil.
- In a medium pot add 4 tablespoons of olive oil and sauté the onion and garlic until glossy. Add the tomatoes, salt, pepper and cook until the sauce is reduced to half. Add the spearmint, remove from heat and leave the sauce cool a little.
- Place a layer of aubergines in a baking pan, evenly spread the crumbled Feta cheese and the sauce over them.
- Place the baking pan in a preheated oven and bake for 20 minutes at 180°C.

The dish can be eaten both hot and cold. It tastes amazing and is ideal for a first course in a formal meal.

Tsakonia in Leonidio produces the best aubergines in the world. They are deep purple with white streaks. If you find them, choose them. They can be cooked in various ways. They make an excellent appetizer in the oven with Feta cheese from Tripoli.

CHICKPEAS
with tomato sauce and cauliflower

for 5-6 people

Ingredients

- *250 g chickpeas*
- *1 large onion, grated on the grater*
- *¼ cup olive oil*
- *1 cup grated tomato*
- *1 tablespoon tomato paste*
- *650 g cauliflower*
- *1 teaspoon ground cinnamon*
- *½ teaspoon ground allspice*
- *1 tablespoon sugar*
- *1 tablespoon vinegar*
- *salt, freshly ground pepper*

- Soak the chickpeas in water overnight. The next day rub them between your hands to remove the skins, wash them well and leave them in a colander.
- Cut the ends of the cauliflower into small florets and wash them well.
- In a large pot, heat the olive oil and gently sauté the onion. Add the chickpeas and continue sautéing.
- Add the grated tomato, the tomato paste dissolved in 1 cup of water, the cinnamon, allspice, sugar, vinegar, salt and freshly ground pepper.
- Lower the heat and cook with the pot covered for 1 hour, until the chickpeas are tender. If necessary, add a little lukewarm water.
- Add the cauliflower, turn up the heat and cook for about 15 minutes. Uncover the pot and continue cooking until the cauliflower softens and the sauce thickens.
- Serve in soup dishes.

"GIANT" *beans in the oven*

for 6 people

Ingredients

- *1 kg giant beans*
- *½ kg sausage of Kalamata*
- *2 large onions, grated on a grater*
- *4 cloves garlic, grated*
- *3 tablespoons tomato paste*
- *1 can of coarsely chopped tomato*
- *1 cup olive oil*
- *1 tablespoon sugar*
- *1 tablespoon sweet paprika*
- *1 tablespoon black pepper*
- *1 tablespoon oregano*
- *salt*

- Soak the beans overnight in a basin with plenty of cold water. The next day, strain them and boil them in a pot with plenty of water until soft.
- In the meantime, prepare the sauce: Heat the olive oil in a pot and sauté the onion with the garlic until glossy. Add the boiled beans and stir. Dissolve the tomato paste in 3 cups of water and pour it into the pot.
- Add the chopped tomato, stir and bring to a boil. Add the sugar, salt, paprika, pepper, oregano and cook for only 10 minutes.
- Cut the sausage into 2 cm pieces.
- Put the beans into a baking pan, pour the sauce over them, mix well and spread the sausage.
- Cover the baking pan with parchment paper and cook for about 1 hour at 180°C.
- Remove the parchment paper and continue cooking for 15 minutes, until a crust forms on top.
- Serve hot and accompany with a good hard cheese.

You can make this recipe without the sausage, to be completely vegetarian.

"HILOPITES" *noodles* *with Feta cheese, oregano and fresh tomatoes*

for 4 people

Ingredients

- *1½ cup of fine 'hilopites' noodles*
- *2 cups grated tomatoes*
- *1 onion, grated*
- *¼ cup olive oil*
- *1 teaspoon grated oregano*
- *15 pitted Kalamata olives*
- *150 g Feta cheese*
- *salt, pepper*

- In a medium saucepan, heat the olive oil and sauté the onion until glossy.
- Add the noodles, oregano, Kalamata olives and grated tomato, stirring continuously.
- Pour in 1 cup of hot water, lightly salt and pepper well.
- Stir frequently with a wooden spoon, so that the food does not stick.
- When the noodles have absorbed most of the juice, turn off the heat, cover the pot and let them absorb all the liquids.
- Just before serving, crush the Feta cheese with the fork, add it to the pot, stir and serve on a platter.

The 'hilopites' noodles are a traditional handmade pasta made all over Greece, with variations from place to place.

TSILADIA *fish*

for 6 people

Ingredients

- *1 large fish (dusky grouper, common dentex, white grouper) about 1½-2 kg*
- *3 large onions, sliced into rounds*
- *3 garlic cloves, finely chopped*
- *2 tomatoes, cut into rounds*
- *1cup fresh tomato juice*
- *1 cup black raisins*
- *2-3 bay leaves*
- *1 cup olive oil*
- *salt, pepper*

- In a large frying pan, heat the olive oil and sauté the onion with the garlic, until glossy. Add the tomato juice and boil for 5 minutes. Pour in the raisins and stir.
- Put the tomato slices in a deep pot and place the fish on top of them. If the fish is large, cut it in half.
- Add the bay leaves, season with salt and pepper and, if necessary, add a little lukewarm water, until the fish is almost covered.
- Cook over low heat until the sauce thickens and the oil rises to the surface.
- Let the food cool a bit and serve.

The recipe is also great with salted cod.

The word "tsiladia" is possibly a paraphrase in Greek of the words "of oil".

LALAGIA

for 1 large tray

Ingredients

- *1 kg all-purpose flour*
- *¾ cup olive oil*
- *1 sachet dry yeast*
- *salt*
- *some lukewarm water*
- *oil for frying*

- Put the flour with the oil in a bowl and knead until a crumbly dough is formed. Add the salt and knead again.
- Dissolve the yeast in ¼ cup of water, pour it into the flour mixture and mix. Add enough lukewarm water to form a soft dough that doesn't stick to the hands. Cover it with plenty of towels and let it rise for about 1 hour.
- Transfer the dough onto a lightly floured surface, knead for a while and cut into large balls. Roll each ball into a cord. Cut the cord in 3 pieces and form each piece into a ring, joining one end with the other.
- Add plenty of olive oil in a deep frying pan and as soon as it is hot, fry the lalagia for 1-2 minutes on all sides until golden brown.
- Drain the lalagia on a rack and serve plain, with cheese or honey.

Lalagia are oil rusks that are fried in plenty of olive oil and stay crispy and delicious for a long time.

RECIPES
from
DODECANESE

The Dodecanese are another cluster of Greek islands, in the southeast borders of the country.

Rhodes, with its magnificent old town and castle of the knights, Kos, the island of the father of medicine, Kalymnos with its sponge divers, Patmos with the sacred monastery of the Apocalypse, and all the other islands, each one offering a small piece of paradise.

The cuisine of the Dodecanese is as special as its islands. Many products have a Protected Designation of Origin and the excellent local dishes owe their flavor to the high quality of their ingredients.

Galeopites from Symi, chickpea fritters from Rhodes, and xerotigana from Leros guarantee many memorable moments of enjoyment!

GALEOPITES *(atherinopites)*

for 2-4 people

Ingredients

- *600 g atherina fish (smelt)*
- *1 grated tomato*
- *1 large onion, grated*
- *¾cup flour*
- *5 eggs*
- *3-4 leaves of spearmint*
- *4-5 tablespoons grated cheese*
- *olive oil for frying*

- In a bowl add the onion, cheese and eggs. Chop the spearmint into pieces and add to the mixture.
- Add the atherina fish, salt, pepper and mix well. Add the flour and stir to form a smooth, not firm, batter.
- Heat plenty of oil in a deep frying pan. Drop spoonfuls of the mixture (making sure that it has fish) in the oil and fry over medium heat on both sides until golden brown.
- Place the fritters for a few minutes on absorbent paper, to drain the oil, and serve.

Instead of atherina, you can use shrimp or any small fish, or even larger fish cut into pieces.

In Symi they also catch a small prawn that is fried in olive oil and becomes crispy and eaten like a roasted almond.

CHICKPEA *fritters*

for 2-4 people

Ingredients

- *½ kg chickpeas*
- *2 tomatoes, grated*
- *1 onion, grated*
- *2 tablespoons dried spearmint*
- *1 cup water*
- *300 g flour*
- *salt, pepper*
- *olive oil for frying*

- Soak the chickpeas in water overnight. The next day rub them between your hands to remove the skins, wash them well and blend them into a pulp.
- Put the chickpea pulp into a bowl, add the onion, spearmint, tomatoes, water and mix. Add the flour and stir again.
- Heat plenty of oil in a deep frying pan. Drop spoonfuls of the mixture in the oil and fry over medium heat on both sides, until the fritters turn golden.
- Put the chickpea fritters for a few minutes on absorbent paper, to drain the oil, and serve.

Use self-rising flour or alternatively add a teaspoon of baking powder to the mixture. The fritters will puff up nicely. Serve them with a tomato salad and an aromatic tzatziki.

CUTTLEFISH *pilaf*

for 4-6 people

Ingredients

- *1½ kg cuttlefish, with their ink*
- *1 large onion, finely chopped*
- *2 garlic cloves, finely chopped*
- *1 small glass white wine*
- *400 g tomato juice*
- *300 g Parboiled rice*
- *1 cup olive oil*
- *salt, pepper*

- Carefully clean the cuttlefish, reserve their ink, rinse and cut into pieces.
- Heat the olive oil in a pot and sauté the onion with the garlic until glossy. Add the cuttlefish and continue sautéing for about 5 minutes.
- Deglaze with the wine and when it evaporates, pour in the tomato.
- Dissolve the ink in a cup of water and strain it. Pour it into the pot with the cuttlefish and stir.
- Bring the food to a boil, add 5 cups of water and add the rice. Stir, season with salt and pepper and simmer until the rice is cooked and the sauce thickens. (If necessary, add hot water.)

Cuttlefish ink, like squid and octopus ink, is a dark pigment whose main component is the melanin protein.

SQUID *with green beans*

for 4-6 people

Ingredients

- *1 kg squid*
- *1 kg green beans*
- *4 onions, grated*
- *2 tablespoons tomato paste*
- *1½ cup olive oil*
- *salt, pepper*

- Clean the squid, rinse them, cut into pieces and leave them to drain.
- Heat the olive oil in a pot and sauté the squid. Add the onions and cook for 10 minutes.
- Add salt, pepper and the tomato paste.
- As soon as the food comes to a boil, add the green beans and 2 cups of water.
- Shake the pot, cover and cook over medium heat for 1 hour.

In Karpathos they often cook seafood with vegetables. A classic recipe is also octopus with spinach.

STUFFED *squid*

for 4 people

Ingredients

- *8 large squid, about 15 cm long*
- *1 cup rice*
- *1 cup tomato juice*
- *2 tablespoons tomato paste*
- *1 large onion, grated on the grater*
- *1 tablespoon dried spearmint*
- *1 cup olive oil*
- *salt, pepper*

You can stuff the squid with a thousand and one ingredients, such as bulgur or even cheese.

- Remove the bone from the squid and wash thoroughly. Cut off the heads, remove the beaks and finely chop the tentacles.
- In a large frying pan, heat half of the olive oil and sauté the tentacles with the grated onion.
- Stir well and add the rice, tomato juice, spearmint, salt and pepper.
- Simmer for 5 minutes, remove from the heat and allow the filling to cool slightly.
- Fill the squid with the mixture (without overfilling) and seal the top with a toothpick.
- Place the squid in a shallow and wide pot. If there is leftover filling, also add it to the pot.
- Dissolve the tomato paste in a cup of water and add it to the pot along with 1 more cup of water to cover the squid.
- Add the rest of the olive oil, a little salt and enough pepper and cook over medium heat for 1 hour, until the squid are tender.

GIOUVETSI
with scorpion fish in the oven

for 6 people

Ingredients

- *2 scorpion fish about 2 kg*
- *½ kg large orzo pasta*
- *1 large onion, grated on the grater*
- *1 cup olive oil*
- *2 tablespoons tomato paste*
- *2 cups tomato juice*
- *1 tablespoon sweet paprika*
- *1 tablespoon turmeric*
- *salt, pepper*

⊙ Heat the olive oil in a pot and sauté the onion until glossy.
⊙ Add the tomato juice, the tomato paste dissolved in 3 cups of water, paprika, turmeric, salt and pepper and mix.
⊙ Bring the sauce to a boil and pour it into a deep baking pan.
⊙ Put the scorpion fish on top, cover with parchment paper and cook in a preheated oven at 180°C for about 45 minutes.
⊙ Remove the parchment paper, add the orzo into the baking pan and cook for 30 more minutes, stirring frequently and gently the orzo in the baking pan

Giouvetsi is a shallow and wide clay pot for baking food in the oven.

XEROTIGANA

for 20-30 pieces

Ingredients

for the syrup
- *2 cups water*
- *1 kg sugar*
- *1 stick of cinnamon*

for the dough
- *1 kg all-purpose flour*
- *1 cup olive oil*
- *1 teaspoon salt*
- *1 teaspoon raki or other distillate e.g. ouzo*
- *olive oil for frying*

for sprinkling
- *roasted sesame seeds*
- *cinnamon*

- Put the water, sugar and cinnamon stick in a pot and boil until the syrup thickens. Remove from heat and let cool.
- Put the flour in a basin, pour in half the olive oil and raki and sprinkle with salt. Stir and pour in the water gradually until you make a somewhat firm dough.
- Knead well, cover the dough with a wet towel, leave it to rest for 1 hour and knead again.
- Transfer the dough to a floured surface and roll out a thin sheet.
- Cut the sheet into 3 cm wide and 6 cm long strips. With each strip, make a small roll.
- Put plenty of olive oil in a frying pan to heat up and fry the xerotigana until golden brown. Take them out with a slotted spoon and place them on absorbent paper to drain the excess oil.
- Dip them one by one in the pot with the syrup, leave in for 2 minutes, take them out with a slotted spoon and drain them on a rack that you have placed over a baking pan.
- When they have drained, place them on a platter and sprinkle with sesame seeds and cinnamon.

RECIPES from CENTRAL GREECE

⊙ ⊙ ⊙

Central Greece, Thessaly, Evia (the country's second-largest island), as well as the lush green Sporades and the emerald islands of the Aegean, coexist harmoniously and feature a rich gastronomic culture.

The fertile plain of Thessaly is the granary of Greece, as fine grains are cultivated there. The smooth tsipouro from Tyrnavos is unique, while the grape varieties *Savatiano* and *Roditis* produce retsina, a very distinctive type of wine.

In the mountains of central Greece, cheesemaking is prevalent and all dairy products, including cheese, yoghurt, and butter, are of exceptional quality.

The beaches, particularly the Messolonghi lagoon, are teeming with fish, but the islands also have a wide array of fine products to offer: the Skyros goat, Alonissos tuna, Kimi figs, olives from northern Evia, plums from Skopelos and so much more.

Authentic, unforgettable recipes, starring pure ingredients and a love for delicious food!

BATZINA *pie*

for 1 baking pan

Ingredients

- *600 g all-purpose flour*
- *200 g green zucchini*
- *150 g fresh milk*
- *180 g olive oil*
- *300 g Feta cheese*
- *salt, pepper*

- Grate the zucchini on a grater and place in a colander. Salt, squeeze well with your hands and let sit for 15-20 minutes to release their liquid.
- In a large bowl, add the zucchini, milk, oil and Feta cheese, crumbled by hand. Stir and begin to slowly add the flour, continuing to mix until a thick batter forms. (If it comes out too liquid, add a little more flour and if it comes out too thick, add a little milk.)
- Grease a large baking pan, pour the mixture into it and spread it evenly.
- Bake in a preheated oven at 200°C for about 40-45 minutes, until the surface turns golden brown.

You can also make this recipe with yellow pumpkin. You can replace all-purpose flour with cornmeal. However, the pie must be thin, up to one centimetre in height.

Batzina is the simplest and tastiest pie you will find in Greece. It is extremely light and can be served both hot and cold.

SKOPELOS *cheese pies*

for 4-5 pieces

Ingredients

- *½ kg Skopelos goat cheese or crumbled Feta cheese*

for the pastry dough

- *1 kg wheat flour*
- *1 tablespoon olive oil and a little more for drizzling on the pastry*
- *1 teaspoon vinegar*
- *a little salt*
- *water*
- *cornstarch for rolling out the pastry*

- Sift the flour in a basin, pour over the oil and vinegar and sprinkle with salt.
- Make a small hole in the middle and gradually add the water, kneading until you form a firm and well-worked dough. Leave it to rest for about 10-15 minutes and divide into balls.
- Sprinkle a surface with plenty of cornstarch and roll out each ball into a thin sheet about 50 cm in diameter.
- Drizzle the pastry sheet with a little olive oil and spread the cheese in the centre of the sheet.
- Roll the pie into a long tube and wrap into a spiral.
- Follow the same process until you are out of dough.
- Fry the cheese pies in plenty of hot olive oil and as soon as they are golden brown on one side, turn them over on the other.
- Place them on absorbent paper to drain the oil and serve hot.

In the northern Sporades they make fried cheese pies with local cheese and xinomyzithra cheese. If you use Feta cheese, then add some myzithra or ricotta to reduce the amount of salt.

LOBSTER PASTA

for 4 people

Ingredients

- *1 package spaghetti No 6*
- *2 small lobsters*
- *2 onions, finely chopped*
- *6 large tomatoes, cut into cubes*
- *4 tablespoons olive oil*
- *12 basil leaves*
- *salt, pepper*

- In a large frying pan heat the olive oil and sauté the onion until glossy.
- Add the tomatoes, season with salt and pepper and cook until the sauce thickens.
- Blanch the lobsters for 10 minutes in boiling salted water, drain them and cut them lengthwise in half with a large sharpened knife.
- Add them to the sauce and cook for 3 minutes with the lid on.
- Boil the pasta in the water where the lobsters boiled and drain.
- Serve the pasta on a platter, drizzle with the sauce and lobsters and garnish with the basil leaves.

The lobsters caught in the Greek seas do not have claws but two long antennae, and their meat is extremely tasty.

TRAHANAS *soup with lamb*

for 6 people

Ingredients

- *1 kg lamb, cut into portions*
- *1 cup sour trahanas*
- *2 tablespoons tomato paste*
- *1 teaspoon chili flakes*
- *salt, pepper*

- Put 2 litres of water in a large pot, salt it and boil the lamb for about 1 hour, skimming it for a clear broth.
- Remove the meat with a slotted spoon, strain the broth, measure about 4 cups and return the broth to the pot.
- Dissolve the tomato paste in it, season with salt and pepper, add the chili flakes and the meat.
- As soon as the food starts to boil, add the trahanas, stirring constantly, and simmer for about 10 minutes. The soup should be thick, almost like pilaf.
- Serve the food hot in soup plates.

Trahanas is made all over Greece, sometimes with flour and milk and sometimes with cracked wheat and milk. They usually let the milk go sour and give it its characteristic taste. Each region has a different name for it. In Mytilene it is called "chachle" and in Crete it is called "chondros" or "xinochondros".

SPETZOFAI

for 4 people

Ingredients

- *½ kg country-style sausage, cut into 1 cm long slices*
- *10 green cow-horn peppers or 3 colored peppers*
- *600 g ripe tomatoes, passed through the purée mill*
- *1 cup olive oil*
- *salt, pepper*

- Cut the peppers and remove the seeds.
- Put half the oil to heat in a frying pan and lightly fry the peppers until soft.
- Remove the peppers from the pan, add the remaining oil, put in the sausages and sauté them until golden brown.
- Add the peppers, pour in the tomato and simmer until the sauce thickens.
- Serve the food hot.

You can also add aubergine pieces to the food, after first frying them, but also 1-2 cloves of garlic, if you like its taste.

Spetzofai is a traditional recipe of the Pelion region and the sausage used can also be made with beef meat.

COD *"plaki"*

for 4 people

Ingredients

- *4 fillets salted cod, well soaked to remove the salt*
- *¼ cup olive oil*
- *2 onions, cut into matchsticks*
- *20 black pitted olives*
- *¼ cup capers, soaked to remove the salt*
- *4 pickled cucumbers, cut into rounds*
- *2 cups tomato juice*
- *salt, pepper*

⊙ Mix the tomato juice, olives, capers, cucumber and olive oil in a bowl.

⊙ In a baking pan spread the onions, place the cod on top and pour the tomato mixture over them.

⊙ Cover the baking pan with parchment paper and bake in a preheated oven at 170°C for about 20 minutes. Remove the parchment paper and continue baking for another 10 minutes at 200°C.

If you want, you can add potatoes, to make the dish more filling.

Salted codfish is a "national" food of Greece, as no table goes without it on March 25th, the anniversary of the Greek revolution against the Turkish yoke.

RECIPES
from
IONIAN ISLANDS

A cluster of verdant islands and one of the most beautiful areas of the country.

The Ionian cuisine is heavily influenced by the Venetians and includes a variety of vegetables, legumes, grains, fish, and seafood.

Corfu is known for its kumquats, the small aromatic citrus fruit, Zakynthos for its mandoles (roasted and caramelised almonds), and Lefkada for its lentils from Eglovi and its salami. Kefalonia is famous for its meat pie, Ithaca for the dishes baked in tserepa, a clay pot that renders them especially delicious.

Here the flavors remain unchanged over time, offering a unique gastronomic experience!

MEAT *pie*

for 1 baking pan

Ingredients

- *1 kg hogget lamb or mutton without bone, cut in very small pieces*
- *½ cup brown rice for pilaf*
- *3 garlic cloves, finely chopped*
- *1 large onion, grated on the grater*
- *¼ cup parsley, finely chopped*
- *1½ cup canned coarsely cut tomatoes*
- *some fresh marjoram, finely chopped or dried ground marjoram*
- *1 teaspoon cinnamon*
- *1 teaspoon ground allspice*
- *¼ cup olive oil*
- *salt, freshly ground pepper*
- *1 package country-style phyllo pastry*

- In a large frying pan, heat the olive oil and sauté the onion and garlic until glossy. Add the meat and continue sautéing until the liquids are absorbed. Add the canned tomatoes, cinnamon, allspice, marjoram, salt and pepper. Add the rice and stir. If the filling is too dry, add some water. Remove from heat and let cool.
- Grease a baking pan, place 3-4 pastry sheets well brushed with oil, making sure that the edges protrude from the sides of the pan. Spread the filling evenly, turn the edges of the pastry inwards, cover with another 3-4 sheets and seal the edges well.
- Carve the pie, drizzle with a little olive oil and bake in a preheated oven at 180°C for 1 hour.

The most magnificent dish of Kefalonia. The recipe differs in its details from house to house and from village to village. What always remains constant is the meat that goes inside: the Kefalonians insist on saying that the best is the hogget lamb.

Hogget is a 1 year old lamb which has not yet given birth.

PASTITSADA

for 6 people

Ingredients

- *1 rooster around 2 kg, cut into portions*
- *150 ml olive oil*
- *1 large onion, grated on the grater*
- *4-6 garlic cloves*
- *1 tablespoon tomato paste*
- *1 tablespoon vinegar*
- *1 tablespoon sugar*
- *1 teaspoon allspice grains*
- *1 teaspoon sweet paprika*
- *1 teaspoon cinnamon*
- *4-5 cloves*
- *½ kg pasta No 2*
- *200 g Kefalotyri cheese or permezana cheese, grated*
- *salt, freshly ground pepper*

- In a large pot, heat the olive oil and sauté the rooster on all sides until golden brown. Add the onion and garlic and continue sautéing.
- Dissolve the tomato paste in 2 cups of water and pour it into the pot. Add the vinegar, sugar, cinnamon, allspice, cloves, paprika, salt and freshly ground pepper.
- Lower the heat, add some water if needed, and cook for about 1 hour until the rooster is tender.
- Meanwhile, boil the pasta and strain it.
- Remove the rooster from the pot, add ¼ cup water, bring to a boil, put the pasta in and stir until coated with the sauce.
- Serve the pasta on a platter, put the rooster on top and sprinkle with plenty of grated Kefalotyri cheese.

A food red as the fire, delicious and exceptionally aromatic due to the spices.
Pastitsada can also be made with beef. Prefer brisket or shank.

SOFRITO

for 4-5 people

Ingredients

- *1 kg beef cut into thin slices*
- *1 cup olive oil*
- *8-10 garlic cloves, finely chopped*
- *1 cup parsley, finely chopped*
- *1 cup vinegar*
- *salt, freshly ground pepper*
- *flour for coating*

- Season the meat with salt and pepper and flour it well.
- Put the olive oil in a pan to heat and fry the meat on all sides until golden brown.
- Place half the meat in a medium-sized pot, add half the garlic on top and sprinkle with half the parsley. Put in the rest of the meat and repeat the process.
- Drizzle the food with the vinegar and simmer until the meat is tender, adding hot water if necessary.
- Serve with mashed potatoes.

Do not be afraid of too much vinegar. It is perfectly balanced with the cooked garlic that has become sweeter. In Corfu, they some times put in more than 3-4 heads, but in the recipe we reduced the quantity a lot.

CHICKEN *in the tserepa*

for 6 people

Ingredients

- *1 chicken, cut into portions*
- *1½ kg potatoes, cut into wedges*
- *3-4 tomatoes, grated*
- *5-6 garlic cloves, finely chopped*
- *1 bowl parsley, finely chopped*
- *½ teaspoon oregano*
- *1 teaspoon thyme*
- *juice of 2 lemons*
- *1 cup olive oil*
- *coarse salt*
- *pepper*

- Put the tomatoes, garlic, oil, 1 teaspoon pepper, 2 teaspoons salt, parsley and lemon juice into a baking pan and mix. Add the chicken pieces and mix with your hands to coat with the sauce everywhere.
- Add the potatoes, cover with a second baking pan and bake in a preheated oven at 180°C for about 1 hour until the meat is tender.

Tserepa is a clay lid, which they use to cover the metal baking pan.

LENTILS *soup*

for 6 people

Ingredients

- *1 kg lentils from Eglovi*
- *1 onion*
- *3 garlic cloves*
- *3 bay leaves*
- *1 tablespoon turmeric*
- *¼ cup olive oil*
- *salt, pepper*
- *optionally, 1 grated carrot*
- *vinegar*

Lefkada is famous for the lentils it produces on the plateau of Eglovi. They are very flavorful and are cooked in a special way by the residents of Eglovi. The same recipe can be made with other lentils.

- Rinse the lentils well with plenty of cold water.
- Peel the onion and with a knife carve a cross on the side of its root.
- Peel the garlic cloves and cut in half.
- Put the lentils in a pot, and add water up to at least 3 cm above the lentils.
- Add the onion, garlic, bay leaves, turmeric, pepper and olive oil.
- Once the food starts to boil, lower the heat and cook for 45 minutes.
- Try them, and if the lentils are still hard continue cooking, adding as much water as needed until it becomes a thick soup.
- Serve the lentils hot, drizzling 1-2 tablespoons of vinegar into each dish.
- Accompany with salted sardines, mackerel or bonito and olives.

FISH *savoro*

for 5-6 people

Ingredients

- *1½ kg small fish (whitebait, red mullet or bogue)*
- *220 ml olive oil*
- *220 ml vinegar*
- *5 garlic cloves, finely chopped*
- *1 bunch rosemary*
- *3-4 bay leaves*
- *¾ pack black raisins*
- *all-purpose flour*

- Descale and gut the fish, wash them, let them drain well and dry with absorbent paper.
- Salt the fish, flour and fry for 3-4 minutes on each side.
- Remove the fish from the pan and put them on a platter.
- In the remaining oil, sauté the chopped garlic, add the remaining ingredients and deglaze with the vinegar. Let the sauce simmer for a while and then pour it over the fish.
- Serve the food hot.

Savoro is a dish made everywhere in Greece. However, this particular recipe with raisins can be found only in the Ionian Islands.

Savoro is a way of preserving fish, since rosemary and vinegar keep the food unchanged for days.

BOURDETO

for 5-6 people

Ingredients

- *1½ kg fish for boiling (Scorpion fish or grouper)*
- *¼ cup olive oil*
- *1 large onion, finely chopped*
- *5 garlic cloves*
- *200 g sweet paprika*
- *2 tablespoons tomato paste*
- *some oregano or thyme*
- *salt, pepper*

- In a large saucepan, heat the olive oil and sauté the onion and garlic along with the sweet paprika.
- Stir, add the oil, the tomato paste and continue stirring.
- Add the fish, season with salt and pepper, sprinkle with oregano or thyme and add a little water, until the fish are half covered.
- Cook with an open lid for about 15 minutes until the fish are tender and the sauce thickens.

If you want, you can also add potatoes, to make the dish more filling.

You can also cook octopus or large squid using this method. The recipe owes its colour to paprika and not to the tomato paste. In fact, in Corfu they often don't use any tomato.

COD *with white sauce*

for 5 people

Ingredients

- *1.8 kg salted cod, well soaked to remove the salt*
- *2 medium onions, finely chopped*
- *6 garlic cloves*
- *¼ cup olive oil*
- *3 cups water*
- *5-6 potatoes, cut into slices*
- *some oregano*
- *juice of 1 lemon*
- *salt, pepper*

- Put 1½ cups of water in a large pot, add the olive oil, onion, garlic and bring to a boil.
- Once it starts to boil add the potatoes, sprinkle with the oregano and boil for about 20 minutes, until you can pierce them with a fork.
- Place the cod on top so that all the potatoes are covered. Add some water, season with salt and pepper and cook for 15-20 minutes, until the fish is cooked through.
- Pour the lemon over the food, bring to a boil and serve.

The codfish arrived in Greece when traders from the Peloponnese started to exchange it for raisins!

RECIPES from EPIRUS

A vast coastline with stunning beaches, lakes, rivers, and distinct mountains. In these mountains, where sheep and goats graze, their flavorful milk is transformed into delectable cheeses such as *Feta* and smoked *Metsovo*.

The rich soil of Epirus gives aromatic herbs and greens, used to make delicious pies. It is no coincidence that there are more than 150 recipes for pies in Epirus. However, their most famous dish is pork with leek and celery, with the unique 'avgolemono' sauce.

Fish and seafood play a dominant role in the cuisine of the area, with the famous Amvrakikos shrimp and sardines.

Tasty creations that speak to the heart and soul of every foodie!

CHEESE *pie*

for 1 baking pan

Ingredients

- *1 package phyllo pastry*
- *4 tablespoons fresh butter*
- *4 tablespoons flour*
- *1-2 litres milk*
- *2 eggs*
- *200 g Feta cheese, crumbled*
- *1 cup Kasseri cheese, grated*
- *¼ cup Parmesan cheese, finely grated*
- *1 pinch nutmeg*
- *salt, pepper*
- *olive oil for brushing the pastry*

- Prepare the béchamel sauce: Melt the fresh butter in a large pot and add the flour. Stir with a whisk and lower the heat. Add the milk gradually, stirring constantly until the mixture thickens to a cream.
- Remove the pot from the heat and add the eggs, lightly beaten, stirring briskly. Add the Feta cheese, Kasseri cheese, Parmesan cheese, and mix well.
- Grease a baking pan with oil and spread 4 phyllo sheets, oiling them one at a time, making sure that the edges protrude from the sides of the pan. Spread the filling evenly, turn the edges of the leaves inwards and spread another 4 sheets on top, also oiling them one by one.
- With a knife, carve portions deep into the pie and bake it in a preheated oven at 170°C until the top and bottom sheets are golden brown.
- Remove the baking pan from the oven and when the pie cools down a little, cut it into portions and serve.

PASTA *pie*

for 6 people

Ingredients

- *1 package puff pastry*
- *200 g spaghetti No 6*
- *150 g ham, finely chopped*
- *3 cups smoked Metsovone cheese, grated*
- *2 eggs*
- *¼ cup milk butter*
- *olive oil for brushing the sheets*

- Boil the spaghetti in plenty of salted water and drain.
- In a bowl, mix the melted butter, eggs, cheese and ham.
- Pour the mixture into a pot, add the spaghetti and mix well.
- Grease a round 28 cm mould, cut the puff pastry sheets into long 4 cm wide strips, and put them in the mould in a fanning pattern, placing one end at the centre and outwards, so that half the strip hangs outside the mould.
- Pour the pasta mixture evenly into the pan and turn the protruding strips inwards.
- Bake in a preheated oven at 180°C for about 1 hour, until the puff pastry becomes crispy and golden brown.
- Remove the mould from the oven, allow to cool for a bit, unmould and serve on a platter.

If you want to add a little colour to your pasta, brush the surface with an egg yolk, beaten with a little water.

PIE *with greens*

for 1 baking pan

Ingredients

- *1 pack of country-style phyllo pastry*
- *500 g Feta cheese, crumbled*
- *1 kg spinach*
- *½ kg chard*
- *1 bunch chervil*
- *1 bunch spring onions*
- *1 bunch dill*
- *1 cup olive oil and a bit more for brushing on the pastry sheets*
- *2 eggs*
- *salt, pepper*

- Clean and wash the spinach, chard, chervil or coriander and spring onions very well.
- Boil the greens for 10 minutes in a little water. Strain them and when cool, cut into thick pieces.
- Put the greens, Feta cheese, spring onions, olive oil, eggs, salt and pepper in a bowl and mix well until the mixture is homogeneous.
- Grease a medium baking pan and spread 5 sheets, oiling them one at a time, making sure that the edges protrude from the sides of the baking pan.
- Spread the filling evenly, turn the edges of the sheets inwards and spread another 5 sheets on top, oiling them one by one.
- Carve the pie into pieces and bake in a preheated oven at 180°C for 1 hour, until golden brown.

If you can't find chervil, you can use some coriander and some fresh oregano.

OCTOPUS *bourdeto*

for 6 people

Ingredients

- *1 medium octopus*
- *1 kg potatoes, cut into wedges*
- *¼ cup vinegar*
- *½ teaspoon cayenne pepper*
- *½ teaspoon sweet paprika*
- *2 tablespoons tomato paste*
- *4 garlic cloves*
- *3 bay leaves*
- *1 cup olive oil*

- Put 2 cups of water in a pot and add the octopus whole. Add a little vinegar and boil for 20 minutes.
- Remove from the heat, take out the octopus and cut it into pieces.
- Return the octopus back into the pot, add the two types of pepper, garlic, bay leaves, tomato paste, dissolved in 2 cups of water, olive oil and let it boil for about 40 minutes.
- Add the potatoes and cook for another 30 minutes or so, until the food absorbs its liquids.
- Serve the food hot.

[*The word "bourdeto" is Italian and means "broth".*]

MEATBALLS *with leeks*

for 4-6 people

Ingredients

- *1 kg minced beef*
- *2 medium onions, grated*
- *2 slices stale bread*
- *1½ kg leeks*
- *2 red peppers*
- *olive oil*
- *juice of 2 lemons*
- *salt, pepper*

- Soak the bread, squeeze it well and crumble it with your hands.
- Wash and cut the leeks into thick slices. Wash the peppers, remove the seeds and cut them into large pieces.
- Put the minced meat, onions, 1 tablespoon olive oil and the bread in a bowl, season with salt and pepper and knead well. Put the mixture in the refrigerator for 1 hour.
- Put the leeks in a frying pan with a little water until softened. Take them out with a slotted spoon and put them in a baking pan.
- Add the peppers, 1 cup of olive oil, lemon juice, season with salt and pepper and mix all the ingredients.
- Shape the meatballs and place them on the leeks and peppers.
- Bake in a preheated oven at 170°C for 45 minutes.

If you like, you can add plenty of oregano and 1 tablespoon of tomato paste to the meatballs.

PORK *with leeks and celery*

for 4 people

Ingredients

-1 kg pork leg, cut into portions
- 1 onion, grated
- 1 garlic clove, grated
- 1 cup white wine
- 2 tablespoons tomato paste
- 10 sticks celery, cut into pieces
- 4 leeks, cut into rounds
- salt, pepper
- nutmeg
- olive oil
- juice of 2 lemons (optional)

- In a deep pot, heat the olive oil and sauté the meat on all sides until golden brown.
- Add the onion, garlic, deglaze with the wine and wait a few minutes until the alcohol evaporates.
- Add the tomato paste, dissolved in 2 cups of water, salt, pepper, nutmeg and cook for 45 minutes.
- In another pot heat water, put in the celery and leeks and blanch for 5 minutes. Remove them and add them to the pork.
- Season with salt and pepper and cook for about 1 hour until the meat is tender.
- Optionally you can add the juice from 2 lemons at the end.
- Serve the food hot.

RECIPES from MACEDONIA and THRACE

Tall mountains, dense forests, and a massive coastline that begins from Evros and reaches the west of Thessaloniki.

The cuisine of Macedonia and Thrace has influences from the numerous people who have coexisted there peacefully throughout history, reflected in its extreme diversity. All across the region, there are numerous shellfish and fish farms and everyone loves fish and seafood. On the other hand, mountain populations love meat and cook it in a thousand and two ways. The dairy products are rich and the cheeses and cold cuts excellent.

Two very special spices are produced here, the 'boukovo' hot chili flakes and the world renowned saffron of Kozani. Also famous are its potatoes, rice, as well as the red Florina peppers, which are exceptional pickled. Especially popular are the peaches and crispy cherries. And when we refer to the region's sweets, we must not forget the 'bougatsa', a unique and delectable pie!

So get ready for a journey full of colors, smells and authenticity!

STEAMED *mussels*

for 4 people

Ingredients

- *1½ kg of fresh mussels in their shells, well cleaned and washed*
- *1 bottle of white aromatic wine*
- *1 pinch (½ g) of saffron*
- *1 cup parsley, finely chopped*
- *salt, pepper*

- Add the mussels to a large pot with plenty of water, and boil for 5 minutes. Remove them from the pot and keep only the ones that have opened.
- In another pot, add the mussels and the wine.
- When it comes to a boil, add the saffron, season lightly with salt and add plenty of pepper.
- Cover the pot and cook for 5 minutes.
- Serve the mussels in a deep platter, pour their sauce over them, sprinkle with chopped parsley and accompany with fresh bread.

Steamed mussels are a very popular dish in the coastal areas of Macedonia, where there are several mussel farms.

PASTIRMA *pies*

for 12 pieces

Ingredients

- *3 country-style phyllo pastry sheets*
- *12 thin slices pastirma*
- *6 slices of tomato, cut in half*
- *12 slices Kasseri cheese*

- Cut the phyllo sheets into 12 square pieces.
- Place a slice of pastirma, half a slice of tomato and a slice of Kasseri cheese in each square.
- Wrap into rolls, brush them with a little oil and bake them in a preheated oven at 180°C until golden brown.
- Accompany with a refreshing yoghurt dip with spearmint leaves.

To get the edges of the dough to stick together, brush them with a little water.

Instead of country-style phyllo, you can use other phyllo pastry and fry the pastirma pies in olive oil.

CABBAGE *rolls*

for 6 people

Ingredients

- *1 large cabbage, about 1½ kg*

for the filling

- *600 g minced pork*
- *1 cup rice for pilaf (carolina)*
- *1 large onion, pulped in the food processor*
- *¼ cup parsley, finely chopped*
- *1 cup olive oil*
- *salt, pepper*

for the avgolemono (egg-lemon) sauce

- *2 eggs*
- *juice of 1½ lemon*
- *salt, pepper*

- Remove the outer leaves of the cabbage and carve out its stem with a knife.
- Place the cabbage into a pot with the cut out part downwards, add water until ⅔ of the cabbage are covered and put the pot over medium heat without a lid.
- Simmer for about 7-10 minutes, turn the cabbage upside down, add water and boil for a few more minutes.
- Remove the cabbage from the pot, allow it to cool, remove the leaves one by one and cut the large leaves into half.
- Put the minced meat, well-washed rice, onion and parsley into a bowl. Add ¼ cup water, salt and knead the mixture well. f it is too firm, add a little more water.
- Place each leaf on your workbench, with the curved side downwards, and place a tablespoon of filling in the centre of one end.
- Fold the two ends inwards to secure the filling and roll in. If the leaf is large, cut off any excess.
- Lay a few leaves of the cabbage on the bottom of the pot and place the rolls in layers, next to each other with the joint downwards. Drizzle with the olive oil, place a heavy plate on the stuffed rolls, to keep them in place during cooking, and add lukewarm water until nearly covered.
- Cook for about 40 minutes over medium heat. Then, lower the heat and prepare the egg-lemon sauce.
- Beat the yolks separately from the egg whites and then combine them, folding gently. Add the lemon juice and 6 tablespoons of the broth from the rolls and season with salt and pepper.
- Pour the egg-lemon sauce into the pot and shake it well, holding it by the handles. Leave the food for a few minutes over low heat and serve.

An extremely tasty dish that everyone enjoys. Of course, the recipe differs a lot from place to place. In the region of Kozani they make them with sauerkraut and minced pork.

LEEK *pie*

for 1 large baking pan

Ingredients

for the dough

- *1 kg all-purpose flour*
- *3 tablespoons olive oil*
- *1 teaspoon salt*
- *some cornstarch*
- *lukewarm water*

for the filling

- *1 kg leeks*
- *750 g minced pork, coarsely ground*
- *100 g bacon, cut into small pieces*
- *1 cup dry white wine*
- *1 cup Feta cheese, crumbled*
- *olive oil*
- *salt, pepper*

- Cut the leeks into small rounds and put them with a little water in a frying pan. As soon as they absorb their liquids, pour in the oil and start sautéing. Add the minced meat and finally the bacon. Deglaze the pan with the wine and season with salt and pepper.
- Remove the mixture from the heat, allow to cool for a bit and add the Feta cheese.
- Prepare the dough: Mix the flour, oil, salt and lukewarm water and knead until a relatively firm dough is formed. Cover it and let it rest for half an hour.
- Divide the dough into two parts, transfer to a surface sprinkled with cornstarch and roll out 2 sheets with the rolling pin, one larger than the other.
- Brush the baking pan with oil and place the largest sheet on the bottom, with the edges protruding. Evenly spread the filling and turn the edges of the sheet inwards.
- Cover with the second sheet, carve the pie into portions and brush with a little olive oil.
- Place the baking pan in a preheated oven and bake at 160°C for about 1 hour, until the surface of the pie is golden brown.
- Before taking it out of the oven, you need to pierce it with the fork to allow its liquids to evaporate.

*If you want you can use ready-made phyllo pastry.
In this case, place 3 sheets on the bottom of the baking pan and 3 sheets on the top of it.*

In many regions of Macedonia and Thessaly, the New Year's coin is hidden in the leek pie, which they cut on New Year's eve as the year changes.

MUSSEL *pilaf*

for 4 people

Ingredients

- *1 kg mussels, well cleaned and washed*
- *1 bunch dill, finely chopped*
- *1½ cup 'nihaki' rice (long-grain)*
- *1 onion, sliced into rounds*
- *½ kg tomatoes, grated*
- *olive oil*
- *salt, pepper*

- Place the mussels into a large pot, pour in a cup of water and let them steam. Strain the broth in a fine-mesh strainer and reserve it to use later.
- In another pot, heat the olive oil, sauté the onion until glossy and deglaze with the grated tomatoes.
- Add the dill, the broth you have set aside and 2 cups of water.
- As soon as it comes to a boil, add the rice and stir, being careful not to let it stick to the bottom.
- When the rice is cooked, add the mussels and stir gently. Cover the pot and bring to a boil.
- Turn off the heat, let it settle and serve.

Mussels are rich in antioxidants and vitamins and are low in fat.

ROOSTER
with white sauce and hilopites noodles

for 6 people

Ingredients
- *1 rooster cut into small portions*
- *1 small onion*
- *1 cup olive oil*
- *1 bottle of Moschofilero wine*
- *juice of 1 lemon*
- *1 tablespoon oregano*
- *½ kg country-style noodles*
- *5 tablespoons milk butter*
- *250 g dry Mizithra cheese or Parmezan cheese*
- *salt, pepper*

- Heat the olive oil in a large pot and sauté the rooster with the onion.
- Deglaze with the wine and when the alcohol evaporates, season with salt and pepper.
- Cover the pot and simmer for over 1 hour.
- When the rooster is tender, add the lemon juice, oregano and stir.
- Boil the noodles in plenty of salted water, drain them, return them to the pot and sauté with butter.
- On a large platter, place the noodles in the middle and the pieces of the rooster around them. Drizzle with plenty of sauce and sprinkle with grated Mizithra cheese.

BAKED LAMB *with yoghurt*

for 6-8 people

Ingredients

- *1½ kg lamb, cut into portions*
- *2 onions, grated*
- *1 cup olive oil*
- *1 kg Greek yoghurt*
- *3 eggs*
- *1 cup dill, finely chopped*
- *salt, pepper*

- Heat the olive oil in a large pot and sauté the onion with the lamb.
- Season with salt and pepper and add the dill.
- Stir well, add some water and cook for half an hour.
- Remove the pot from the heat and place the lamb in a baking pan that fits it snuggly.
- Put the yoghurt in a large bowl, lightly season it with salt and pepper, add the eggs and beat well until they are incorporated into the mixture.
- Pour the yoghurt over the lamb and cover the baking pan with parchment paper.
- Bake in a preheated oven at 170°C for at least 1 hour.
- Remove the parchment paper and continue baking until the yoghurt forms a golden crust.
- Serve the food hot.

You can also add peeled artichokes, which you will sauté for a while in the same pot that you sautéed the lamb.

Yoghurt, one of the oldest foods, helps to reinforce the immune system and maintain good health.

RECIPES
from
NORTH AEGEAN

In the north part of the Aegean, there is a cluster of islands, mainly Lesvos, Chios, Samos, Lemnos, Ikaria, and Samothrace, that combine mountain and sea, as well as tradition and tourism. Their products are famous not only in Greece, but also abroad. Lesvos is well-known for its ladotyri cheese and ouzo, Samos for its aromatic wine, Lemnos for its wheat and wine, Ikaria for its seafood-based recipes, and Samothrace for its renowned wild goats.

Mastic, a product extracted from the trunk of a tree that is unique to Chios and used in cooking, confectionery, and alternative medicine, deserves special mention!

Each island has its own unique recipes, and they are all absolutely delicious!

CHICKPEAS *with spinach*

for 4-5 people

Ingredients

- *1 cup large chickpeas, preferably without skins*
- *600 g spinach, cleaned and washed*
- *¼ cup olive oil*
- *juice of 1 lemon*
- *salt, pepper*

- Soak the chickpeas in water overnight. The next day, wash them well and boil them in plenty of salted water until soft, but not mushy.
- Strain them and set aside 2 cups of the water they boiled in.
- Blanch the spinach for 5 minutes in a pot. Strain it and put it in a clean pot, spreading it to cover the entire surface.
- Layer the boiled chickpeas on top so that they cover all of the spinach.
- Add some of the chickpea water, just enough to cover the spinach, and cook over low heat for 10 minutes.
- Take out the spinach and chickpeas with a slotted spoon and place them on a platter.
- Drizzle with the olive oil, lemon, season with salt and pepper and serve.

Alternatively, you can sauté 2 medium onions cut into rounds in a frying pan until golden brown and lay them over the spinach and chickpeas. At the end always add a little lemon juice, salt and pepper.

MEATBALLS *with ouzo*

for 6 people

Ingredients
- *600 g minced meat beef*
- *250 g stale bread*
- *1 large onion, grated*
- *2 eggs*
- *1 teaspoon ground cumin*
- *1½ teaspoon ground oregano*
- *100 ml ouzo*
- *flour for coating*
- *olive oil for frying*
- *salt, pepper*

- Remove the crust from the bread and soak the crumb in water. Squeeze it gently and crumble it with your hands.
- Put the minced meat and bread in a large bowl and mix until the ingredients are incorporated. Add the grated onion and stir again. Add the eggs, cumin, oregano, ouzo, salt, pepper and knead well.
- Cover the mixture and refrigerate for 1 hour.
- Shape into round meatballs, flour them, shaking the excess flour, and fry them in hot olive oil.
- Place the meatballs on absorbent paper for a few minutes and then serve with white rice or fried potatoes.

Optionally, you can add 2 cloves of grated garlic to the minced meat mixture.

If you made too many meatballs and you have leftovers, you can make a spicy tomato sauce the next day, put the meatballs inside and bring to a boil.

Ouzo owes its distinctive taste to the addition of mastic. It accidentally got its name from the inscription "uso Massalia", meaning "for the use of Marseilles"!

STUFFED *onions*

for 1 medium baking pan

Ingredients

- *15 medium-sized onions*
- *250 g minced beef*
- *3 tablespoons 'glacé' (short-grain) rice*
- *¼ cup olive oil*
- *¼ cup dry white wine*
- *2 tablespoons tomato paste*
- *some sweet paprika*
- *1 teaspoon ground allspice*
- *1 teaspoon ground cloves*
- *2 tomatoes*
- *salt, pepper*

For more flavor, you can add some chopped parsley or spearmint to the stuffing.

- Remove the outer husks from the onions and gently carve a cross on top.
- Place the onions in a pot with salted water and boil until tender.
- Remove the onions from the pot and when cool, empty them out carefully with the help of a fork.
- Put the inside of the onions in a food processor to make a pulp and place in a frying pan with hot oil. Add the minced meat and sauté, stirring well.
- Add the rice, allspice, cloves and season with salt and pepper. Deglaze with the wine and as soon as the mixture comes to a boil, add the tomato paste. Stir and remove the pan from the heat.
- Allow the mixture to cool and, with the help of a small spoon, stuff the onions and place them in the baking pan.
- Cut the tomatoes into slices and place them between the onions.
- Sprinkle with paprika and add some water to the bottom of the pan to nearly cover the onions.
- Cover the baking pan with parchment paper and bake in a preheated oven at 170°C for at least 1 hour. Remove the parchment paper and bake for another 15 minutes.

FLOMARIA *with chicken soup*

for 4 people

Ingredients

- *1 whole chicken, well washed*
- *½ kg of flomaria pasta*
- *¼ cup olive oil*
- *200 g Kefalotyri cheese, grated*
- *juice of 1 lemon*
- *salt, pepper*

- Fill a pot with 2 litres of water. Add salt and put the chicken in. If necessary, add water to cover the chicken.
- Cook for about 1 hour and until the chicken is tender and easily falls off the bones.
- Remove it from the pot and cut into portions.
- In the water where the chicken was boiling, add the flomaria and olive oil.
- Simmer the pasta until tender and then add the chicken.
- Cook for 10 more minutes and add the lemon juice.
- Serve a portion of chicken with plenty of pasta on each plate and sprinkle with grated cheese.

You can also make this recipe with macaroni.

[*In Lemnos, they make the twisted pasta which they love so much by hand. They mostly cook them with chicken soup, but also in tomato sauce with beef.*]

PORK SHOULDER *with mastic*

for 4 people

Ingredients

- *1 kg pork shoulder, cut into bites*
- *2-3 tablespoons olive oil*
- *2-3 tablespoons lemon suice*
- *1 teaspoon Chios mastic*
- *1 cup breadcrumbs*
- *salt, pepper*

- Marinate the meat with the oil, lemon and pepper for at least 2 hours in the refrigerator.
- Put the Chios mastic with the salt in a mortar and grind into a powder.
- Pour the crushed mastic with the salt into the breadcrumbs and mix well.
- Take the meat out of the fridge and bread it in the aromatic breadcrumbs.
- Place it in a baking pan and bake in a preheated oven at 200°C for about 35 minutes until golden brown.
- Serve with white rice and garnish with mint leaves.

Chios mastic was the first natural chewing gum of the ancient world and was used for keeping teeth clean.

KATIMERIA

for є people

Ingredients
- 4 cups flour
- 1 cup milk
- 1 cup fresh butter
- 1 cup sugar
- 30 g fresh yeast or 1 sacket of dry yeast
- 3 eggs
- oil for frying (sunflower oil)

for sprinkling
- 2 cups powdered sugar
- 1 tablespoon ground cinnamon

- Dissolve the yeast in ½ cup lukewarm water.
- Gently warm up the milk, put it in a basin and add the dissolved yeast (if you use dry yeast, just add it to the flour).
- Add the sugar, butter, eggs and work all the ingredients together, slowly adding the flour until you have a smocth dough.
- Put the basin in a warm place and allow the dough to rise for about 1 hour until double in volume.
- Knead again and leave the dough in a warm place for another hour.
- Heat the oil in a deep frying pan and drop in small portions of dough with the help of a spoon, frying them until go.den brown.
- Place them on absorbent paper to drain the excess oil.
- Serve the hot 'katimeria' on a platter and sprinkle with sugar and cinnamon.

If you prefer your katimeria savory, you can sprinkle them with a spicy cheese and grated tomato.